An imprint of Rose Publishing, Inc.
Carson, CA
www.Rose-Publishing.com

H. Michael Brewer

This one is for Mom, as promised. And, of course, they're all for Janet.
~ HMB

GOTTA HAVE GOD 2 FOR AGES 10-12

ISBN 10: 1-58411-059-7
ISBN13: 978-1-58411-059-0
RoseKidz® reorder #L46966
JUVENILE NONFICTION/Religion/Devotion & Prayer

RoseKidz®
An imprint of Rose Publishing, Inc.
17909 Adria Maru Lane
Carson, CA 90746
www.Rose-Publishing.com

Cover Illustrator: Dave Carleson
Interior Illustrator: Aline Heiser

Printed in South Korea *14 04.2016.APC*

TABLE OF CONTENTS

TABLE OF CONTENTS

TABLE OF CONTENTS

INTRODUCTION

Nothing is more fun than getting together with a good friend! That's what this book is for, to remind you to spend time with your best friend, Jesus. Do you really need a book to talk to Jesus? Nahhh! But the stuff in this book will give you and Jesus some things to talk about.

So what's in here? There are stories and readings from the Bible to help you get to know Jesus better. There are questions here to think about. (Don't worry! It's not like homework.) And every story has a totally cool puzzle or code or game to give your brain a workout. We put a few easy ones in, but some of these are going to make smoke come out of your ears! Of course, there are answers in the back if you really, really, REALLY need them.

If you're going to use this book, you'd better get the rules straight. The rules are...uh, let's see, there must be some rules. Okay, I've got a couple:

1. Never use a hamster for a bookmark.
2. Do not take this book into the pool. This is not an approved flotation device!

I can't think of any other rules right now, so I guess the rest is up to you. You can read one chapter a day. Or more. Or less. You can memorize the Bible verses. Or not. Or just the ones you like. On the activities and questions, you can use a pencil or a pen or a paintbrush. You can start at the front of the book or the back or in the middle. You can read this book alone with Jesus, or you can get somebody else to share it with you. You're getting the picture, right? Do your own thing.

Wait a minute. I just thought of one more rule. This is the last one, and then I'm out of here.

3. Have fun! After all, you'll be hanging with **Jesus, the best friend anybody ever had!**

Great News

I am wonderful because God made me.

I praise you because I am fearfully and wonderfully made; your works are wonderful.

– Psalm 139:14

Fitness Day

Corey waited for the whistle, then ran the 50-yard dash as fast as he could.

"Not bad," said his physical education teacher, Mr. Grayson. He wrote Corey's time on a card.

"All right, everybody," called Mr. Grayson. "Pair off and do sit-ups. See how many you can do in 60 seconds."

Corey paired up with his friend Manuel. He held Manuel's feet firmly. When the whistle blew, Manuel did sit-ups as fast as he could for one minute. Then they traded places and Corey took his turn. When he finished, they rested and waited for Mr. Grayson to come around and record their scores.

"Ha!" said Manuel. "I did three more sit-ups than you."

"Yeah, but I did two more chin-ups," Corey said. "This is fun."

Manuel said, "Yeah, I like fitness testing day, except for the rope climb. Ugggh! I burned my hands coming down."

"Just look at all this stuff we're doing," Corey said. "Isn't it amazing?"

"What do you mean?"

"Think about everything your body can do," Corey said. "We jump and run and throw and swim and climb."

"Yeah," said Manuel with a grin. "When God made me, God made the best. But when God made you, God made the second best."

"Okay," called Mr. Grayson. "Keep your same partners and keep count for each other for the push-up test."

"Push-ups?" Manuel groaned.

"Now we'll see who's second best," Corey said.

Your Turn

If part of your body didn't work well, would you still be wonderful? Why?

____

____

Prayer

God, I love all the stuff I can do. Thanks for making me who I am! Amen.

GOD'S WONDERFUL WORK

God has made you special, and there is no one else exactly like you. Think of some of the wonderful things about you. On another sheet of paper, write a story about yourself using the words listed below, then share that story with someone who loves you.

Strong	Safe	Challenge
Adventure	Unique	Talent
Excellent	Marvelous	Special
Courage	Good	Learning

GOD AND ME

God loves me no matter what.

How great is the love the Father has lavished on us, that we should be called children of God!

– 1 John 3:1

Love That Can't Be Earned

Troy's dad was driving him to soccer practice. The radio played music from a Christian music station. Between songs, an announcer talked about God's love.

Troy sighed with boredom.

Mr. Parker glanced at his son and said, "God does love you. That's not just something to talk about in church. It's real, you know."

Troy thought about it for a moment.

"Does God love me because I'm captain of the soccer team?" he asked.

"No," said Mr. Parker. "God would love you even if you were lousy at soccer."

"Does God love me because I got an A in Spanish?"

"No. God would love you if you flunked every subject," Mr. Parker said. "Of course, you wouldn't get any allowance for a year. But God would still love you."

"Does God love me because I always do my chores and you never have to ask me twice?"

Mr. Parker raised his eyebrows and looked at Troy.

"Okay, sometimes you have to ask me more than once," Troy laughed.

"God loves you whether you do your chores or not," Mr. Parker said.

"I'm running out of reasons," Troy said. "So why does God love me?"

"Just because you're you and God is God," Mr. Parker said. "God is pleased when you do good things, but those good things aren't the reason God loves you. And doing bad things may disappoint God, but that won't stop God from loving you. God's love is a gift and you can never earn it. God loves you because God wants to."

"Wow!" Troy said.

"Amen!" said the radio announcer.

Your Turn

When you think about God's love for you, how do you feel about God?

___

___

Prayer

God, thanks for all the love. That's the best gift I could ever imagine. Amen.

IF GOD LOVES ME, I MUST BE OKAY!

Cinquain is a kind of poem. It does not have to rhyme. The first line of a cinquain is the title and all the other lines of the poem are about the title. Put your name on the first line and follow the directions to write a cinquain poem about yourself.

Line 1: Write your name.

Line 2: Write two words that describe you.

Line 3: Write three action words that apply to you.

Line 4: Write four feeling words about yourself.

Line 5: Rename the title by thinking of a different word for you.

____

__________ __________

__________ __________ __________

__________ __________ __________ __________

____

GOD AND ME

God proved His love by sending Jesus.

For God so loved the world that he gave his one and only Son, that whoever believes in him shall not perish but have eternal life.
– John 3:16

The Biggest Thing

On the drive home after the soccer game, Troy said, "I've been thinking about God loving me. I believe it, I guess, but I'm wondering how we know for sure."

Mr. Parker thought for a moment.

"There are lots of ways to answer that question, but let me ask you a question first," he said. "How do you know that your mom and I love you?"

"I know you love me because of all the stuff you do for me," Troy said. "You give me a home and food to eat. You buy clothes for me. When I'm sick you take care of me. You drive me all over the place."

"So doing those things for you is one way of proving our love for you, right?" Mr. Parker said. "What about God? What has God done for you?"

Now it was Troy's turn to think.

"God made a beautiful world for me to live in," Troy said. "He has given me a strong body and good health. He gave me a great family and super parents."

"So, all that proves God's love for you," Mr. Parker asked. "But there's even more. God also sent Jesus to show His love."

They drove in silence for a few minutes.

"I can hardly imagine so much love," Mr. Parker said. "I can't think of anything in the world that could make me give up my son, but God loved us so much that he gave up His only Son for us."

"Sending Jesus was the biggest thing God could do for us, wasn't it, Dad?"

Mr. Parker said, "I can't think of anything bigger."

"Neither can I," Troy said.

Your Turn

How do you think God felt about sending Jesus into the world?

____

____

Prayer

God, Your love is higher than the sky and deeper than the oceans and bigger than the world. I'm going to hang on to Your love forever. Amen.

BIG THANKS FOR BIG LOVE

God sent Jesus into the world to show you just how much He loves you. God gives you many things every day to remind you of this great love. In the circles below, write things about yourself, your family, your church and your world for which you are thankful.

Jesus loved me enough to die on the cross for me.

This is how we know what love is:
Jesus Christ laid down his life for us.

– 1 John 3:16

The Ugly Cross

Hasin sat beside Alan in the pew. Hasin was Alan's friend from school. His family had moved from India, and Hasin had never been in a Christian church.

Hasin whispered to Alan, "There on the wall. That's a cross, right?"

"That's right," Alan said. "Most churches have a cross on the wall or on top of the steeple or somewhere."

"Don't be angry," Hasin said, "but isn't that a strange thing to decorate your church with? The Romans used crosses to kill people. A cross is a painful thing."

"We worship Jesus," Alan said, "and Jesus died on a cross. The cross reminds us of that."

Hasin nodded.

"I know that," he said, "but why do you want to remember such a sad story?"

Alan thought about that for a minute.

"Jesus died on the cross because He loves us," Alan said. "He died to take away our sins. He died so we would understand how much God loves us. To us the cross is beautiful because it reminds us of God's love."

"It still seems sad to me," Hasin said, shaking his head.

"It was sad when Jesus died," Alan agreed. "But He's not dead now. He came out of the grave after three days and now He's alive forever."

"Do you believe that?" Hasin asked in surprise.

"Yes," Alan said. "I believe Jesus died and rose again for me."

"Then the story has a happy ending," Hasin said.

"The happiest ending of all," Alan said. He looked at the cross and felt God's love all around him.

Your Turn

Is there a cross anywhere in your church? What do you think of when you see it?

____

____

____

Prayer

Jesus, I can hardly believe how much You love me. You died for me. Help me live for You. Amen.

EASTER EXCITEMENT

Jesus died on the cross, but He rose again. This is great news and you should want to share it with others! Check out the references below and read these Bible stories that tell how people found out about Jesus' resurrection on the first Easter morning. Write the person's name in the blank space that describes him or her.

Thomas Cleopas Mary Magdalene Simon Peter Disciples

1. Read John 20:1-2

When I got to the place where Jesus was buried, I saw the stone had been rolled away from the opening. I ran to tell the disciples that something had happened to Jesus' body.

Who am I? ____________

2. Read John 20:3

Mary told me Jesus' body had been taken from the tomb where He was buried. I ran to the tomb to see what had happened.

Who am I? ____________

3. Read Luke 24:12-16

I was walking from Jerusalem toward the town of Emmaus with another of Jesus' followers. We were talking about all that had happened to Jesus when we were suddenly joined by another traveler. We did not know who he was. We told him all about Jesus and invited the stranger to eat with us. As we began to eat, we realized we had been walking with the risen Jesus.

Who am I? ____________

4. Read John 20:19-20

It was three days since Jesus had been killed. We did not know who had taken His body. We were scared. We were hiding in a locked house when Jesus came and stood in the room with us. Jesus showed us His hands and side. We were so amazed!

Who am I? ____________

5. Read John 20:24-28

I did not believe my friends when they told me Jesus was alive. A few days later, Jesus came to visit us again, and I got to see Him for myself. He showed me His nail-scarred hands and the cut in His side. Then I believed. Jesus is alive!

Who am I? ____________

(The solution is on page 245.)

God loves me even when I mess up.

But if we confess our sins to him, he is faithful and just to forgive us and to cleanse us from every wrong.
– 1 John 1:9 TEV

Never, Ever

When Sunday school ended, the kids filed out of class, but Toby stayed.

"Mr. Murdock," Toby said, "you told us Jesus lives in each Christian."

"That's right," Mr. Murdock said.

"But what if a person kept making mistakes and doing the wrong thing?" Toby asked. "Would Jesus leave?"

The Sunday school teacher smiled and said, "Toby, every Christian makes mistakes. Each morning I decide I'm going to live like Jesus, but by lunchtime I've already messed things up."

Toby had trouble imagining Mr. Murdock messing up.

"What do you do about it?" Toby asked.

"Every night when I go to bed, I think about my day," Mr. Murdock said, "and I tell God I'm sorry for my sins. Then I try to do better the next day."

"That's all?" Toby asked.

"If Jesus lives in you, Toby, then Jesus knows what's in your heart. He knows when you're really sorry and when you're trying to do right."

"And He won't move out of my life?" Toby asked.

"Jesus loves you, Toby. As long as you want Jesus in your life, Jesus will never, ever leave you. Okay?"

"Okay," Toby said. "Thanks, Mr. Murdock."

Toby opened the door and left the room. He was halfway down the hall when he heard Mr. Murdock call his name. Toby turned around and saw his teacher standing in the classroom doorway.

"Never, ever, Toby. He'll never, ever leave you."

Toby smiled and gave his teacher a thumbs-up.

Your Turn

What words do you use to ask God to forgive you?

____

____

Prayer

God, I know Your love is bigger than my sins. Forgive me for my mistakes and help me do better next time. Amen.

THE PRODIGAL CHICKEN?

Jesus told a parable to help us understand that God will forgive us when we make bad choices. You can read the Parable of the Prodigal Son (and his brother) in Luke 15:11-24.

A messed-up version of that parable is below. It has 11 mistakes in it. Cross out the incorrect words and replace them with the correct words to see what Jesus really had to say about forgiveness.

There was a man who had two chickens. The fatter one said to his father, "Father, give me my share of the estate."

So he divided his property between them. Not long after that, the younger son got together all he had, set off for a distant circus and there squandered his wealth in wild living.

After he had spent everything, there was a severe flood in that whole country, and he began to be in need. So he went and hired himself out to a window-washer of that country, who sent him to his pond to feed ducks.

He longed to fill his stomach with the sardines that the pigs were eating, but no one gave him anything.

So he got up and went to his cousin.

But while he was still a long way off, his father saw him and was filled with compassion for him; he ran to his son, threw his arms around him and smacked him.

The son said to him, "Father, I have sinned against heaven and against you. I am no longer worthy to be called your pet dog."

But the father said to his servants, "Quick! Bring the best hat and put it on him. Put a tattoo on his finger and bells on his feet. Let's have a feast and celebrate. For this son of mine was dead and is alive again; he was lost and is found."

(The solution is on page 245.)

God adopted me to be part of His own family.

God was kind and decided that Christ would choose us to be God's own adopted children.

– Ephesians 1:5 CEV

The Family Day Picnic

The Blakes sat on a quilt spread on the green park lawn.

Mr. Blake said, "We are gathered here on Family Day to remember the day Jesse joined our family."

Jesse threw a dandelion at his father and it bounced off Mr. Blake's shoulder.

"Don't be so serious," Jesse said.

"But this is serious business," Mr. Blake said, winking at Jesse. "Seven years ago today we brought you home to be our son."

"I wish I could remember it," Jesse said. "But I was only two years old."

"I remember it," said Jesse's mom. "It was the happiest day of my life. We worked so hard to adopt you and waited so long before it was final."

"What was it like?" Jesse asked, although he'd heard the story many times.

"Well," said Jesse's dad, "there wasn't much to it. Your mom and I went to the baby section of the supermarket. We looked over all the babies and checked the price tags. Then your mom saw you sitting on the shelf and she said, 'Let's take that funny-looking kid.' So we brought you home."

"You're awful," Mrs. Blake told her husband. She turned to Jesse. "We prayed for God to lead us to the right child," she said. "And God helped us find you. Of all the children in the world, you're the one we wanted. We picked you to be part of our family, just the way God picked you to join God's family."

"That's how it was," Mr. Blake agreed. "God led us to the third shelf in the baby department of the supermarket."

Jesse and his mom started throwing dandelions at Jesse's dad. They didn't stop until he surrendered.

Your Turn

All Christians are part of God's family. Who are some of your "brothers and sisters" in God's family?

____

____

Prayer

God, it feels so good to belong to You and Your family. Thanks for choosing me to be Your kid. Amen.

A FAMILY AFFAIR

God gives us different kinds of families. Some people have big families, and others have just a few in their families. Some families like to play games together, and other families like to hike in the woods. God also gives us a bigger family, the family of God's followers. Look at the activities listed on this page. Use a red marker to circle the ones you do with members of your home family. Use a blue marker to circle the ones you do with people from your church family. How many things do you do with both your family and your church family?

WORK

EAT

VISIT PEOPLE

PLAY

REST

SLEEP

STUDY

SING

MAKE DECISIONS

SHARE STORIES

TRAVEL

SHOP FOR THINGS WE NEED

PRAY

HELP OTHERS

GOD AND MY LIFE

God knows where I'm going even when I don't.

Even before I was born, you had written in your book everything I would do.

– Psalm 139:16 CEV

The Big Plan

"Do you ever wonder where you're going to end up?" Mike asked Rodney.

Mike and Rodney were in the stands behind home plate, watching a minor league baseball game. A new batter stepped up to the plate.

"I know where I'm going to end up," Rodney said. "After the game I have to cut the grass. Then I'll shoot hoops until it gets dark."

"I don't mean today," Mike said. "I mean your life. Do you ever worry about where you'll go to college? What job you'll get? Whether you'll get married?"

The batter smacked the ball and both boys jumped to their feet. They cheered as the ball soared over the fence.

"Wow! Did he hammer that or what?" Mike asked.

"Nahhh," Rodney said.

"Are you telling me he didn't hammer it?"

"No, I'm telling you I don't worry about how my life is going to end up," Rodney said. "Oh, you've got to make plans, but I don't worry about it."

"How come?" Mike asked.

"God's in charge, right? The pastor always says that God will make our lives turn out right if we have faith," Rodney said.

"So did God plan for you to paint your shirt with mustard?" Mike asked.

"No, that's just because I'm a slob," Rodney asked. "I'm not saying God has every little thing already settled, like what I'm going to eat for breakfast next Thursday. I'm just saying God loves me and He will make the big stuff work out the way it should."

"Yeah," Mike admitted. "Maybe I think too much."

"I'm thinking I want another hot dog," Rodney said. "How about you?"

Your Turn

Is it easy to trust God to help your life turn out the way it should? Why or why not?

____

____

Prayer

God, I don't know what's going to happen tomorrow, but I know You'll be there to take care of me. Amen.

MEANDERING MOSES

It took Moses 40 years to lead his people through the wilderness to the Promised Land. Sometimes they wandered around, and other times they ran into trouble. But Moses always trusted that God would get them to their new home in Israel. Moses did his best along the way and he trusted God to handle the big stuff. In the end, the people got to Israel just as God had promised.

This winding trail mentions a few of the things that happened while Moses wandered through the desert. For each caption, draw a picture to show what happened. If you want to learn more, look up the stories in your Bible.

Jesus is always right beside me.

And be sure of this: I am with you always, even to the end of the age.

– Matthew 28:20 TEV

Best Friends

Quinn dropped his book bag, grabbed an apple from the kitchen and hurried off to meet his best friend at their favorite place. After a short walk, Quinn reached the quiet spot where the creek created a small pool under the trees.

Quinn settled on his favorite rock and said to his friend, "Man, I love it here."

Quinn and his friend sat in silence, listening to the gurgle of the water.

"What a great day in school," Quinn said. "First, the missing library book turned up. I knew I had returned that book. The librarian found it on the wrong shelf or something, and now I won't have to pay for it."

Quinn took a bite of his apple.

"Then I got my English back, and I aced it! I got a 92. You know what? I kind of like poetry."

Quinn worked on the apple for a while.

"You'll never guess what we did in gym class today," Quinn said. He grinned and added, "Well, maybe you already know. We played crab ball. That is my game, even though it gives me blisters on my palms."

They sat without talking, the way good friends sometimes do. Quinn flicked pebbles into the pool, smelling the sweet spearmint and enjoying his friend's company. At last, Quinn stood up and brushed his pants clean.

"Thanks for meeting me here," Quinn said to Jesus. "I know You're with me all the time, but I still like to tell You about my day. Come on. We'd better hurry or I'm going to be late for dinner."

Anyone watching Quinn walk toward home would have thought he was alone.

But he wasn't.

Your Turn

Even though Jesus is always with you, do you think He likes to hear about what's going on in your life? Why or why not?

____

____

Prayer

Jesus, You are always with me, and that is so amazing. Help me remember that I can talk to You any time and any place. Amen.

VISITING WITH JESUS

Imagine Jesus has come to visit you today. Draw a picture of yourself (in the center circle) with Jesus. What would you want to tell Him? Write something in each circle that you want to tell Jesus.

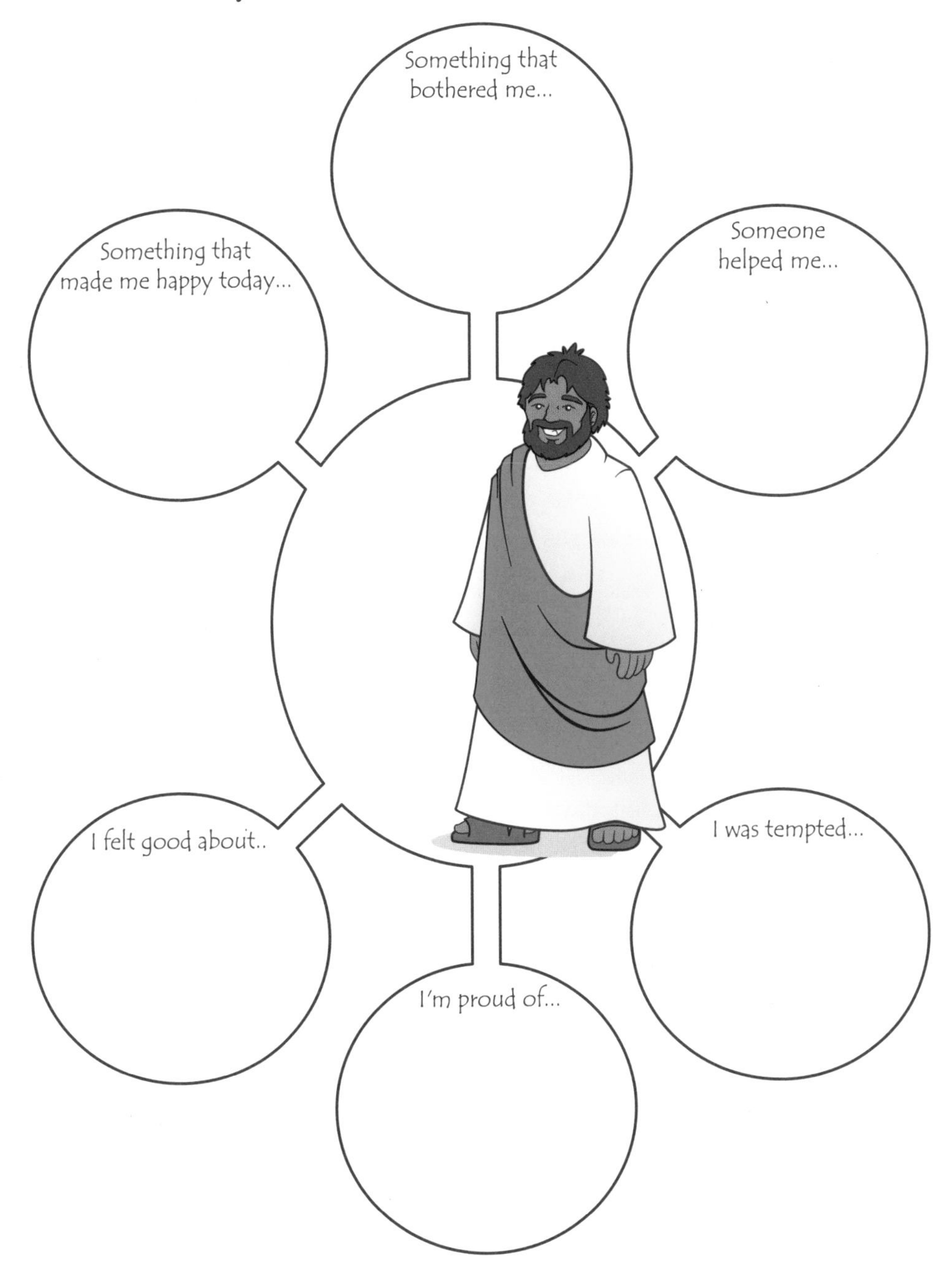

GOD AND MY LIFE

God provides for me every day.

Your heavenly Father already knows all your needs and he will give you all you need from day to day if you live for him.

– Matthew 6:32-33 TEV

Tough Times

"Why so sad today?" Mrs. Stark asked her son Greg.

She laid a slice of toast on his plate. Greg spread jam on his toast.

"I heard you and Dad talking," Greg said. "Are we going to run out of money?"

Mrs. Stark sat down at the table and picked up her coffee cup.

"We don't have much left in the bank," Mrs. Stark said. "Your father's been laid off from work for months now. And so far your father hasn't found a job."

She sipped her coffee.

"I'm not getting many hours at the drugstore," Mrs. Stark said. "I might have to look for another job, too."

"I heard Dad say we might have to move out of this house," Greg said.

"Maybe," Mrs. Stark said. "We could save some money if we moved to a small apartment. Or we could even move in with Grandpa for a while."

"I'm scared," Greg said, staring at his plate. "What if we can't buy groceries? Will we starve?"

Mrs. Stark reached out and gently lifted her son's face. She looked into his eyes.

"You don't have to be scared," she said. "Your father and I have been in hard times before, and God has always taken care of us. God will do it again."

Mrs. Stark squeezed her son's hand.

"Quit worrying," she said. "It's a beautiful sunny day, and God's going to give us everything we need today."

"What about tomorrow?" Greg asked.

"If God's big enough to handle today," said Mrs. Stark, "then we can let God handle tomorrow when it gets here."

Your Turn

What is the difference between what you want and what you need?

____

____

Prayer

God, I know You've been taking care of me! If You'll take care of me again today, I won't worry about tomorrow. Amen.

A.S.K.

When you have needs, Jesus says to bring those needs to God. You can use the initials A.S.K. as a reminder to turn to God for everything you need.

ASK for what you need. SEEK God's help. KNOCK on His door with prayer.

What will happen if you A.S.K. God? Decipher what Jesus says. To figure out the message, read the grid coordinates. Fill in the letters on the blanks. The first number in a coordinate is always the bottom number. For instance, 2,5 is L.

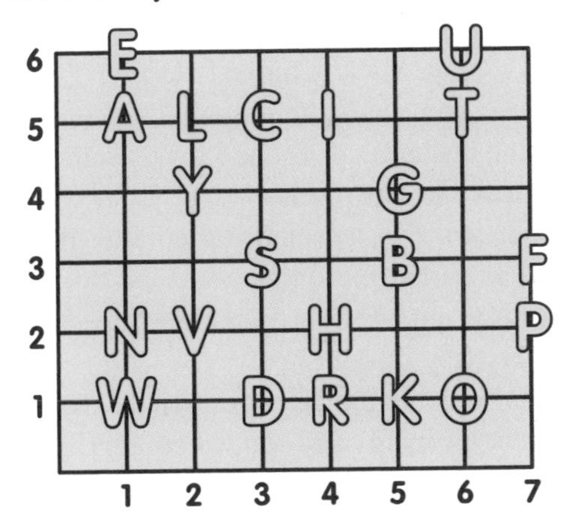

1,5 3,3 5,1   1,5 1,2 3,1   4,5 6,5   1,1 4,5 2,5 2,5

5,3 1,6   5,4 4,5 2,2 1,6 1,2   6,5 6,1   2,4 6,1 6,6;

3,3 1,6 1,6 5,1   1,5 1,2 3,1   2,4 6,1 6,6

1,1 4,5 2,5 2,5   7,3 4,5 1,2 3,1;

5,1 1,2 6,1 3,5 5,1   1,5 1,2 3,1   6,5 4,2 1,6

3,1 6,1 6,1 4,1   1,1 4,5 2,5 2,5   5,3 1,6

6,1 7,2 1,6 1,2 1,6 3,1   6,5 6,1   2,4 6,1 6,6.

(The solution is on page 245.)

GOD AND MY LIFE

God always keeps an eye on me.

Do not be dismayed, for I am your God. I will strengthen you and help you; I will uphold you with my righteous right hand.
– Isaiah 41:10

24/7

Mickey saw a young robin sitting in the bushes near the porch. The bird was small and seemed scared. Mickey moved closer.

Maybe the bird needs some help, he thought.

He squeezed into the bushes and reached for the little bird, but the baby cheeped and hopped away into the yard.

Mickey wiggled out of the bushes and started after the young bird. Suddenly a shrill call came from a nearby tree. Mickey looked up. A fully-grown robin sat on a low branch. The bird squawked again and swooped out of the tree to land between Mickey and the baby bird.

Mickey decided that was the mother bird. Mickey took a step forward and the mother bird fluttered her wings and squawked angrily. At that moment, Mickey heard another call from behind. A second adult robin sat on the edge of the roof glaring at Mickey. The father of the baby bird!

"Okay," Mickey said, laughing. He backed away from the young bird. "Settle down. I'm not going to hurt your baby."

Mickey returned to the porch. The father flew back to the roof to keep watch. The mother cocked her head for a moment, then plucked a worm from the soil. She dropped the worm into the mouth of the baby, who gobbled it up eagerly.

Mickey decided the baby bird was going to be okay. Even though he hadn't seen the parents at first, they were nearby watching over their child.

Just like God, Mickey thought. *Even when I forget God is nearby, He is still keeping a close eye on me because I'm His child.*

Your Turn

Do you think God ever loses you or forgets about you? Why or why not?

___

___

Prayer

Thanks, God, for watching over me 24/7. I know You'll never let me down. Amen.

UNDER GOD'S PROTECTION

We talk about the eyes and ears and hands of God, although we know God is a spirit. It's easier for us to think about God if we imagine God having body parts as we do. Sometimes the Bible describes God with body parts we don't have. Like what? Decipher this passage and you'll find out. You'll also be reminded of how faithfully God watches over you.

To read this verse, move each letter backward one place in the alphabet. For example, B becomes A and K becomes J.

IF XJMM DPWFS ZPV XJUI IJT

____ ________ ________ ______ ________ ______

GFBUIFST BOE VOEFS IJT XJOHT

__________, ______ _________ ______ __________

ZPV XJMM GJOE SFGVHF.

______ _________ _________ ___________ ~ Psalm 91:4

(The solution is on page 245.)

GOD AND MY LIFE

God always listens when I pray.

We are certain that God will hear our prayers when we ask for what pleases him.

– 1 John 5:14 CEV

The Lost Game

"I'm not going to pray anymore," Terry said as he and his twin brother, Perry, walked home after the game. "It's just a waste of time."

"How do you figure that?" Perry asked.

"I prayed for our team to win this game so we could go to the district, and we lost anyway," Terry said. "Either God wasn't listening or God doesn't care."

Perry shook his head.

"I know we're twins," Perry said, "but I must have gotten most of the brains. Do you know how goofy you are?"

"I don't care what you say," Terry told him. "I prayed and God didn't give me what I wanted. So I say prayer doesn't work."

"God isn't going to give you everything you ask for," Perry said. "What if you prayed for somebody's house to burn down? Do you think God would do that?"

"But I didn't pray for something bad," Terry said. "I just prayed for our team to win."

"And that's the same as praying for the other team to lose. That wouldn't be fair. Maybe the other team worked harder and practiced longer. Besides, if we could get anything we wanted by just praying, we'd all be lazy and spoiled. Don't you think God wants us to work for things? That's how we grow and get better. God loves you too much to give you things that are bad for you."

"I still say God should have answered my prayer," Terry insisted.

"God did answer you," Perry said. "'No' is an answer. Next time try praying for something you really need, and see if you get a different answer."

Your Turn

Do you believe God listens to every prayer? How does that make you feel?

____

____

Prayer

God, I ask You for lots of stuff, but I know You'll only give me the things that will be truly good for me. Thanks for giving the right answer to every prayer. Amen.

THE JESUS WAY TO PRAY

Jesus gave The Lord's Prayer as an example of how we should pray. Read Matthew 6:9-13, then match the following statements to the parts of the Lord's Prayer each statement describes. (There is more than one match for each statement.)

_____1. We ask for God's help to do the right things.

_____2. We think about the relationships we should have with God and with other people.

_____3. We believe God is concerned about us and will give us what we need.

_____4. We remember to praise and honor God. All power and glory belong to Him.

a. Our Father in heaven, hallowed be your name,

b. your kingdom come, your will be done on earth as it is in heaven.

c. Give us today our daily bread.

d. Forgive us our debts, as we also have forgiven our debtors.

e. And lead us not into temptation, but deliver us from the evil one.

(The solution is on page 245.)

Jesus makes a home in my life.

On that day you will realize that I am in my Father, and you are in me, and I am in you.

– John 14:20

Cleaning House for Jesus

Mr. Murdock said to his Sunday school class, "If Jesus was moving into your house, what would you do to get ready?"

"We'd clean out the guest room," Toby said.

"Good," said Mr. Murdock. He wrote that on the chalkboard. "What else?"

"Weed the garden," one girl said.

"Finish painting the porch."

"Wash all the windows."

As Toby listened to the answers, he thought of some videos and books his family would throw out. They weren't so bad, but you wouldn't leave them lying around if Jesus was visiting.

The answers kept coming until the board was full.

"That's a long list," Mr. Murdock said. "I guess you'd really want your house to look its best if Jesus was going to live there."

Mr. Murdock sat down. "Now I have another question," he said. "What would you do to get ready if Jesus was coming to live in you? Not your house, but you. What would you do to get yourself ready?"

Nobody said anything. Mr. Murdock went on.

"What thoughts would you clean out? What habits would you change?"

No more lying, Toby thought. He'd stop being angry at his English teacher. He'd spend more time reading his Bible and less time watching horror movies.

"Guess what?" Mr. Murdock said. "If you're a Christian, Jesus does live in you. Jesus makes His home in your life."

Toby thought of Jesus living in him. It gave Toby a good feeling to know Jesus loved him so much. But he decided it was time for some spring-cleaning.

Your Turn

What part of your life could you change to make Jesus feel more at home in you?

____

____

Prayer

Jesus, thanks for living in me. I'm glad You know all my secrets and still love me anyway. Amen.

DETOUR AHEAD

Have you ever been traveling in a car when you saw a sign that said "Detour"? A detour sign means you have to make a change in the route you are taking. You might even have to go in a different direction for a while. Sometimes life is like that, too.

Here are some examples from the Bible where people's lives needed to change in order for them to follow Jesus. Look up and read the stories in your Bible, then create a road sign for each person. It doesn't have to be a real road sign–just put a few words or a picture on that sign to show the kind of change that person is going to have to make.

Paul (Acts 26:12-18) Simon Peter and Andrew (Mark 1:16-18)

Zacchaeus (Luke 19:1-8) Rich Young Man (Luke 19:16-22)

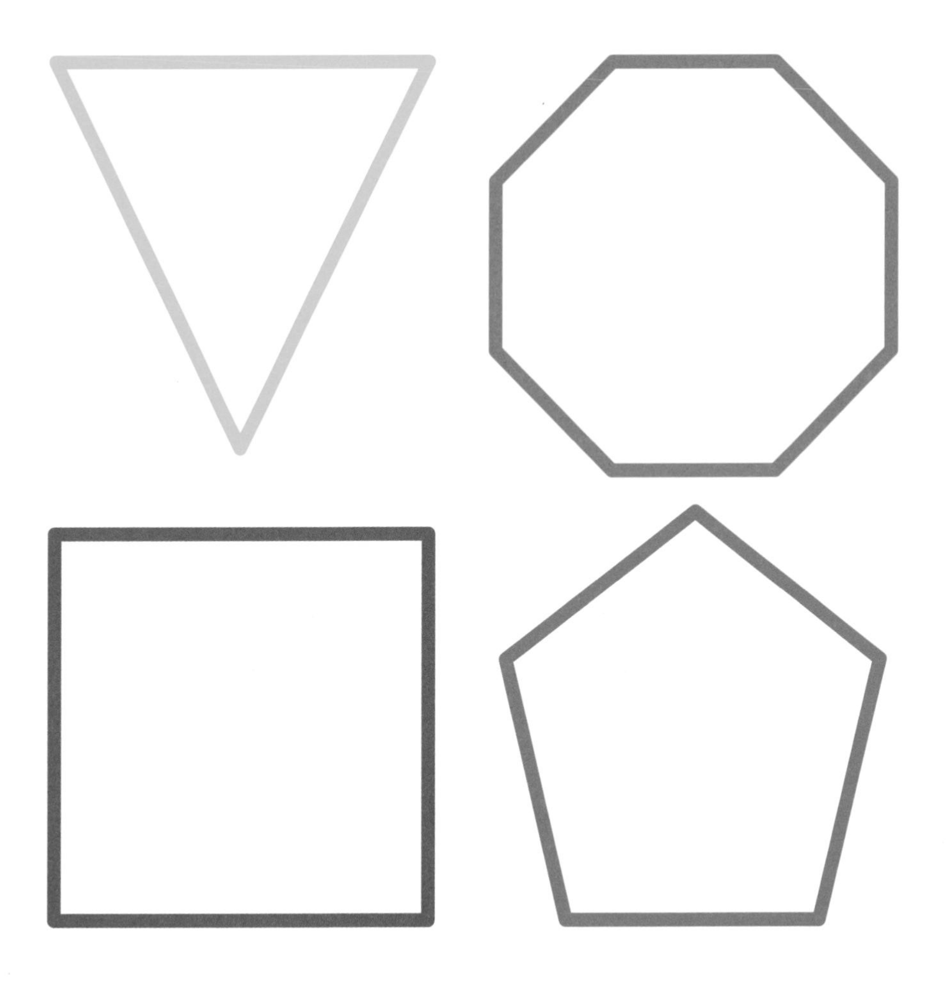

FEELING GOOD ABOUT ME

RESPECTING MYSELF

God wants me to take care of my body.

Do you not know that your body is a temple of the Holy Spirit, who is in you, whom you have received from God? You are not your own; you were bought at a price. Therefore honor God with your body.

– 1 Corinthians 6:19-20

God's Gift

"You smoke?" Grant asked in surprise as Steve took a pack of cigarettes from his pocket. Steve was new in school and Grant hadn't known him long.

"It's no big deal," Steve said. "Do you want one?"

"No way," Grant said. "Smoking trashes your health."

"It's my body," Steve said with a shrug.

"Not exactly," Grant replied. "You like to draw, right? Say you spent days on a beautiful ink drawing and you gave it to me as a present. How would you feel if I scribbled on it or left it out in the rain?"

"I'd be hurt, I guess," Steve said. "So what?"

"Your body is a gift from God," Grant said. "God made it just for you. How do you think God feels when you mess up His gift?"

"I never thought of that," Steve said, looking uncertainly at the unlit cigarette in his hand.

"Maybe you should," Grant said. "Think of the great stuff you might do with your life. What a shame to mess everything up because you didn't take care of your health."

"I haven't been smoking very long," Steve said, hesitating. "Maybe it wouldn't be that hard to stop."

"Now you're talking," Grant said and slapped Steve on the back. "Let's find a trash can and put those cigarettes where they belong."

Your Turn

When you think about God's Spirit living in you, how does it make you feel about yourself?

____

____

Prayer

Thank You for this incredible body, Lord. Amen…and wow!

TAKING CARE OF THE GIFT

God makes all kinds of bodies. Yours is special because God made it, and God doesn't make junk! When you take care of your body and protect your health, you give honor to our Maker. The pictures below are reminders of some of the ways you can help or hurt your body. Draw an X through the ones that disrespect God's gift, and draw a heart around each one that honors God.

I can't fool God or myself.

I know, my God, that you test the heart
and are pleased with integrity.

– 1 Chronicles 29:17

No Fooling

Mr. Jordan said, "Before I hand out the test, please put away all your books and notes."

Peter nervously fingered the cheat sheet tucked inside his sleeve. Peter had never cheated before, but he couldn't figure out this biology stuff. The only way to ace this test was with a little hidden help, he had decided.

Mr. Jordan looked at the class. "You will be taking two tests today," he said. "One test in biology and one in integrity. Will you choose to be a biologist when you grow up? Probably not. But what kind of person do you want to be? Trustworthy? Honest? Will you take pride in your work and earn your success? Your choices today will shape your character tomorrow."

As Mr. Jordan handed out the tests, he said, "You might be able to cheat without getting caught. Maybe I'll never know, and neither will your parents. But you'll know."

The folded-up paper felt like a rock in Peter's sleeve. He slipped it into his book bag and zipped it out of reach.

I'm not a cheater, he told himself. *That's not who I want to be.*

Peter looked at the test. It was harder than he'd expected.

Even if I get a bad grade, Peter thought, *at least I'll know it's the grade I earned on my own. And God will know, too.*

Your Turn

"Integrity" means doing the right thing even when no one is watching. Can you think of a time you did the right thing even though no one knew about it?

____

____

Prayer

Lord, I want to make You proud of me. Help me do the right thing even if You and I are the only ones who notice. Amen.

PASSING THE TEST

It's not always easy to be our best selves. This secret message from Psalm 119:11 tells us one way to protect ourselves from temptation.

Each letter in the message below is one letter off in the alphabet. For instance, M is either L (the letter before M in the alphabet) or N (the letter after M in the alphabet). Put the right letters in place to figure out the lesson.

J IBUF IJCCFM XPTS VNSE JO LZ GDBQS SIBU

__ ____ ______ ______ ____ __ __ _______ _____

H NJFGS MNS TJM BFBHOTU ZNV

__ ______ ____ ____ _________ ____.

(The solution is on page 245.)

RESPECTING MYSELF

When I make a promise, I need to keep it.

Who may worship in your sanctuary, Lord?
Who may enter your presence on your holy hill?
Those who...keep their promises even when it hurts.

– Psalm 15:1, 4 NLT

The Pool Date

Hamadi danced around the living room playing air guitar. He was totally excited. In a radio contest, Hamadi's friend Brady had won tickets to the Kicking Parrots concert on Saturday. Brady had invited him to go to the concert.

Hamadi's father called from the basement, "Please turn that music down!"

As Hamadi lowered the music, he overheard his little brother, Musa, on the telephone in the kitchen.

"Yeah, Hamadi is taking me to the pool Saturday. I can hardly wait."

Oh, man, Hamadi thought. *I forgot all about taking Musa swimming. We'll just have to make it a different day. He won't mind.*

"He's already called it off twice because he had other things he wanted to do," Musa continued. "But he promised we'd go this Saturday for sure."

Musa went on, "We'll take sandwiches and snacks and spend the whole day at the pool. It'll be great. Hamadi's the best big brother in the world."

This is so unfair, Hamadi thought. *When I made that promise I didn't know I'd get a chance to see the Kicking Parrots on Saturday. The pool will be there all summer, but the Parrots will only be in town for one day.*

Musa listened for a minute then said, "No, he won't forget. He promised."

Hamadi settled on the couch and stared at the ceiling. This swimming trip was really important to Musa. If Hamadi broke the date again, Musa might think Hamadi cared more about the concert than he did about his little brother.

When Musa hung up the phone, Hamadi went to the kitchen and called Brady to tell him he wouldn't be able to go the concert. Something more important had come up!

Your Turn

Have you ever made a promise and wished you could take it back? What did you do?

____

____

Prayer

Lord, You keep all Your promises. Help me to be like You and keep the promises I make, even when it's hard. Amen.

ROCK STEADY

God is a promise maker and a promise keeper! When God makes a promise, you can stand on it like a solid rock. God never breaks a promise. Never! Below are a few people to whom God made promises. Can you match the person on the left with the correct promise on the right? If you need help, look up the stories in the Bible.

Abraham (Genesis 12:6-7)	"I will give you wisdom."
Sarah (Genesis 18:9-10)	"I will help you defeat the Midianites."
Moses (Exodus 3:7-8)	"I will make you as strong as an iron pillar."
Joshua (Joshua 1:5)	"I will bring my people out of Egypt."
Gideon (Judges 6:14-16)	"I will not leave you or forsake you."
Jeremiah (Jeremiah 1:17-19)	"I will give you a land of your own."
Solomon (1 Kings 3:10-12)	"I will give you a child."

(The solution is on page 245.)

RESPECTING MYSELF

I can praise God with my words.

Nor should there be obscenity, foolish talk or coarse joking, which are out of place, but rather thanksgiving.

– Ephesians 5:4

The New CD

Billy Garrick's mother pounded on the door of his bedroom and asked, "What in the world are you listening to?"

Billy pushed the pause button on his CD player and opened his door.

"It's my new CD, Mom. You said I could buy it."

"Maybe I did," Mrs. Garrick said, "but I didn't know it had that language."

"Sorry, Mom," Billy said. "I'll use my headphones."

"No, I don't want you listening to that kind of music," Mrs. Garrick said.

"But, Mom!" Billy protested. "Everybody has this CD!"

"Billy," Mrs. Garrick said, "I know you want to listen to the same music as your friends, but some of this music isn't good for you. Just like everything else in life, words are a gift from God. Instead of using words in ugly ways, God wants us to use our words to encourage others and to praise Him."

"I'm not using those words," Billy said.

Mrs. Garrick held up her hand to stop his argument.

"I understand that," she said. "But when you bought that CD, you gave your money to the people who made it. You were saying: 'I like these dirty words. Keep it up!'"

Billy looked miserable.

"I guess you're right," he said.

"I'll go with you to the store and we'll get your money back for this CD. I don't care if it is already opened," Mrs. Garrick said. "When I explain the problem to the manager, he might give you a refund. Then we'll shop for another CD. With all the music out there, I know you can find something you like that won't fill our house with ugly words."

Your Turn

What are some ways you can use words to please God?

____

____

Prayer

God, I want every part of me to serve You, including my mouth. Help me use words that show Your goodness. Amen.

WAYS TO PRAISE

The Bible gives us lots of words and phrases that we can use to praise God. Go around these word wheels skipping every other letter to find some of them. Write the words you find in the blanks below.

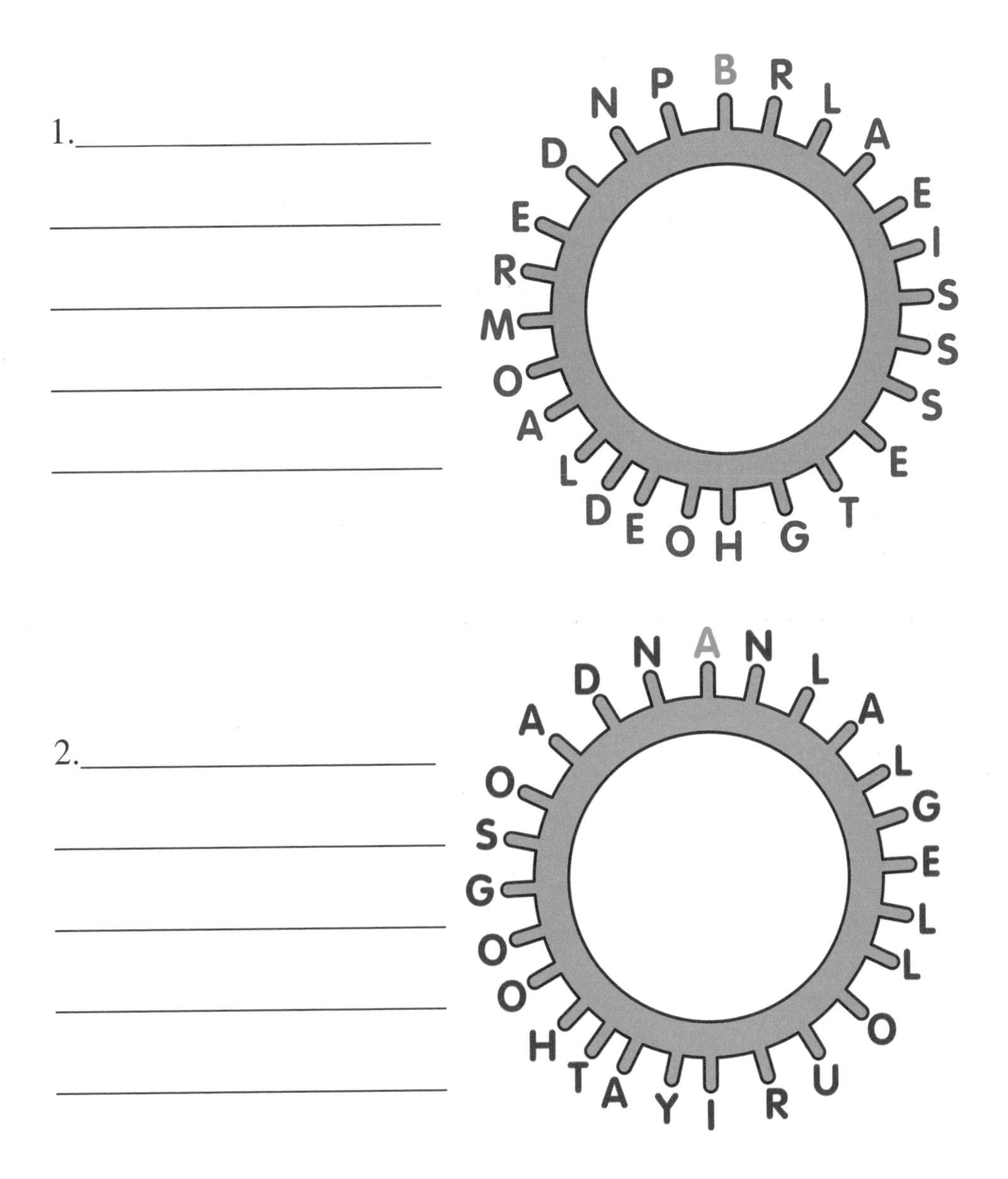

(The solution is on page 245.)

God wants me to do my best at every job.

Whatever your hand finds to do, do it with all your might.
– Ecclesiastes 9:10

The Grass or the Game?

"We're going to miss the game," Harris said.

Tyler paused in sweeping the grass clippings from the driveway and looked around the big yard. He usually mowed Mrs. Queen's grass on Thursday, but this week's rain had forced him to postpone the job until Saturday.

"I'm not finished yet," Tyler told his friend.

Harris pointed to his watch impatiently and said, "That's good enough. Let's get going."

Tyler said, "I still have to trim around the bushes, and there's a few places I ought to rake."

"It's just grass!" Harris protested. "What's the big deal if you take a few shortcuts? Mrs. Queen won't know if you skip the trimming."

"I'll know," Tyler insisted. "I'm the one who asked for this job. When Mrs. Queen hired me I promised I'd do it right."

"But you're the best fielder on the team," Harris pleaded.

"Do you know what makes me a good fielder?" Tyler asked. "When I'm playing ball, I don't goof around. I give it my very best. Whenever I do something I try to do it as well as I possibly can. That includes baseball, homework, chores and cutting grass!"

Harris shook his head and climbed on his bike.

"Get to the park as soon as you can," he called as he rode off.

"I'll be there when I finish this job," Tyler said. "As soon as I finish it right."

Your Turn

When you look at the world around you, do you think God takes pride in doing good work? Why?

____

____

Prayer

Lord, I want to do a good job even when the job is no fun. Help me do my best every time. Amen.

FINISHING THE JOB

If God had hurried through the job of creation, things might not have been finished correctly. Imagine a cat with one cow's leg, or a fish with a wing! Finish the incomplete pictures on this page as you remember to finish the jobs you start…and finish them right.

DOING MY BEST

The harder I try, the further I will get.

Perseverance must finish its work so that you may be mature and complete, not lacking anything.

– James 1:4

The Free Throw

When Buddy walked to the free-throw line, the crowd shouted and cheered like crazy. He bounced the ball a few times and looked at the basket. Gradually, the noise died down. The gym became quiet while Buddy concentrated on the shot.

The whole game was riding on Buddy now. Only two seconds were left on the scoreboard. The score was tied and Buddy had one foul shot coming. If he made this basket, his team would win.

Buddy glanced at his coach on the sidelines. The coach smiled and nodded. He seemed to be saying, "Go for it."

The coach always told his team that they worked hard in practice so that the games would come easy. Buddy tried to live up to that. He spent hours practicing free throws, lobbing one ball after another, over and over and over. The coach called that "perseverance."

Buddy rolled the word around in his mouth: perseverance. It meant hanging in there. It meant practicing and practicing. It meant not quitting, not getting discouraged, not throwing in the towel. Perseverance meant making up his mind to become the best free-throw shooter on the team, and then working hard to make that come true.

Yeah, Buddy decided, I've definitely got perseverance. I've probably shot a thousand free throws to get ready for this shot. Nobody's ever perfect. I might miss today, but if I do I'll just go practice some more.

He raised the ball, rose on his toes, and lofted the ball toward the basket. It cleared the rim and dropped cleanly through the net!

Your Turn

Do you find it hard to keep trying when things don't come to you right away? Why or why not?

___

___

Prayer

God, some of the things I want in life aren't going to come easy. Give me the strength and perseverance to keep working for what I really want. Amen.

HANG IN THERE

Sometimes it's hard to keep trying when everything and everyone seems to be working against you. But you can know God will help you keep your promises and do the things you need to do if you depend on His strength. Complete the following sentences as reminders to turn to God for help when things get tough.

I will trust God to help me hang in there when

My parents want me to...

____

I am embarrassed by...

____

I have trouble learning to...

____

My friends don't understand why...

____

My brother/sister is mean to me because...

____

DOING MY BEST

Making plans helps me succeed.

The wise look ahead to see what is coming,
but fools deceive themselves.

– Proverbs 14:8 NLT

Getting Smart

Jay looked over his grades and felt proud. Four B's and two A's. Excellent! And it was all because of his planning book!

Jay had always worked hard in school, but his grades weren't very good because he was so disorganized. He remembered one weekend when it felt like his world was crashing down on him. He was supposed to clean out the garage by Sunday night or he'd lose his allowance. He had also made plans to go to the movies on Saturday, but then he remembered that his science project was due Monday. The project was a big part of his grade. And he'd promised to help the church youth group with a food drive on Sunday afternoon.

Jay panicked. He cancelled the movie and his friends got mad. He cleaned the garage, but he did a lousy job and still lost his allowance. He explained to his youth group leader that he wouldn't be able to help with the food drive and felt guilty about it. He spent Sunday on his science project, but the project stunk, and Jay felt lucky to get a C-minus.

That terrible weekend convinced Jay to get organized. He bought a calendar and made it his planning book. He wrote down every assignment and its due date, and he included church events, plans with friends, chores and family activities.

It wasn't easy to make new habits, but soon Jay's grades improved. He learned to plan ahead and use his time carefully. Now Jay wondered how he ever got by without his planning book!

He opened the book to today's date and wrote:

Show my grades to Mom and ask for my favorite dessert!

"Now there's a plan!" he said.

Your Turn

What can you do to help yourself plan ahead?

____

____

Prayer

God, You give us all the same amount of time. Help me be smart in how I use mine. Amen.

FORKS IN THE ROAD

Planning your life is a little like planning a road trip. On a trip, every time you come to a fork in the road you have to make the correct turn if you want to reach your destination. Life also brings forks in the road called "choices." Life will turn out for the best when you know where you want to go, and when you make the right choices to get yourself there.

Here are some choices that you may face sometimes. The destination is at the bottom of the fork and the choices are on either side. Choose the road that you believe will lead to the desired destination and trace that course with a marker. Notice that sometimes the destination is fun–there's nothing wrong with having fun in life! Just remember that fun isn't ALWAYS the best choice.

Call friends the day before to make plans.

Sleep late on Saturday and hope somebody will drop by.

A fun Saturday

Do homework on the bus on the way to school.

Do homework right after dinner each night.

Good grades

Put off lawn work as long as possible.

Mow grass a day early if it looks like rain.

Do chores on time to get allowance

GROWING

Growing is God's plan for me.

Jesus grew in wisdom and stature, and in favor with God and men.

– Luke 2:52

More than Inches

Rashid stood straight while his father measured him against the door frame. On every birthday, Rashid's father made a new notch to show that year's growth.

"You're almost an inch taller than last year," Rashid's father told him.

"Is that all?" Rashid said with disappointment. "I'm the third shortest guy in my class. Why am I growing so slowly?"

"I'm not very tall, Rashid," his father reminded him, "and neither is my father. Maybe you take after us."

"Great," Rashid mumbled. "I'll probably never grow up."

Rashid's father laid his hands on his son's shoulders and looked at him.

"Rashid, there's more to growing than just getting taller."

"Like what?" Rashid asked.

"For your birthday last year I gave you a pair of in-line skates. Remember?"

"Sure," said Rashid, his eyes lighting up.

"And do you remember how you kept falling when you first tried them out?"

"Yeah, but now I can out-race anybody in the neighborhood and I've learned to do all sorts of skating tricks."

"And last year," his father continued, "you barely passed math. But this year you've brought your grade up to a B."

"Hey, that's right," Rashid agreed.

"What about your guitar? You're playing real songs now."

Rashid rubbed the calluses on his fingertips and thought about how many chords he had learned.

His father smiled and squeezed Rashid's shoulders.

"In all the important ways, Rashid, you've grown at least a foot this year!"

Your Turn

Name at least three ways you hope to grow in the year ahead.

____

____

Prayer

God, You have packed me full of possibilities. I can't wait to see what You're going to make of me! Amen.

GROWING IS MORE THAN ADDING INCHES

There are lots of ways to grow. Sometimes your decisions and choices show that you are growing in ways that make God happy. In each of the pairs of statements, one choice will help the person grow, the other will not. Circle the statement that shows a choice to grow into the kind of person God wants you to be.

Dylan pretended to be sick so he could watch extra TV.

Matt helped his dad rake leaves.

Rod offered to help his little brother start his science experiment.

Keith cancelled a movie date with his little brother in order to play baseball with friends.

John explained to Scott how he had broken Scott's scooter and then offered to pay for the repairs.

Jeff broke Scott's scooter, but told Scott he didn't know how it got broken.

Tim went to the movies with friends and didn't get his math homework finished.

Kevin told his friends he couldn't go to the movies because he had to finish his homework.

Real strength doesn't need big muscles.

Finally, be strong in the Lord and in his mighty power.

– Ephesians 6:10

Getting Stronger

Jason's father had taken off his shirt on this warm day. He was a big man. Every time he swung the axe, muscles moved in his arms and back. With each swing the axe bit into the roots of the old tree stump and wood chips flew into the air.

Jason's father laid the axe aside and pushed against the stump. It rocked, but only a little. Jason's father sat down on the stump and Jason sat beside him.

"Do you think I'll ever be as big as you?" Jason asked.

"Oh, sure," his father said. "Look how big your feet are! You're going to be a tall man. You'll pass me up one of these days."

"But will I be strong?" Jason persisted.

"Strong isn't the same as big," Jason's father said. "Strong is up to you. Some people think strong is about how much weight you can carry or how hard you swing a hammer, but that's nothing."

Jason's father pulled a red bandanna from his pocket and wiped his face.

"Listen to me, Jason. Strong is about being a man. And being a man means keeping promises. Taking care of your family. Walking away from a fight whenever you can. Respecting people, especially women. Honoring the Lord."

Jason's father smiled at his son.

"Son, I've seen the way you hold the door open for your mom. I've seen you stand by your friends. I know you took up for your little brother when he was getting pushed around," Jason's father said. "You're going to be a strong man. You're already stronger than some men I know."

Jason's father gave him a sweaty hug, then asked, "Are you ready to try out this axe?"

Your Turn

Why was Jesus a strong man?

____

____

Prayer

Lord, I know muscles aren't enough to make me a real man. Give me strong love and strong faith so I can be a strong man. Amen.

THE ARMOR OF GOD

Paul told the early Christians to be strong in the Lord and in God's power by putting on the armor of God. Here is what Paul says about that armor.

"Therefore take up the whole armor of God, so that you may be able to withstand on that evil day, and having done everything, to stand firm. Stand therefore, and fasten the belt of truth around your waist, and put on the breastplate of righteousness. As shoes for your feet put on whatever will make you ready to proclaim the gospel of peace. With all of these, take the shield of faith, with which you will be able to quench all the flaming arrows of the evil one. Take the helmet of salvation, and the sword of the Spirit, which is the word of God." (Ephesians 6:13-17 NRSV)

Find each piece of armor Paul describes and write the full name in the correct spaces in the picture below.

(The solution is on page 245.)

GROWING

God helps me to be strong when I'm tempted.

And God is faithful; he will not let you be tempted beyond what you can bear.

– 1 Corinthians 10:13

The Growling Belly

As Barrett watched television his stomach began to growl. When a commercial came on, Barrett went to the kitchen for something to eat. The coach had told Barrett he needed to lose a few pounds, but losing weight wasn't easy.

"Just lay off the sweets between meals," the coach had told him. "That will do it."

Barrett was trying, but he loved snacking. In the kitchen he found a chocolate pie. Anything chocolate was his favorite. Mom had probably baked the pie for dessert after tonight's dinner, but why wait? Barrett could have a piece now and another for dessert.

As he got out a plate and reached for a knife, he heard his coach's words again. "Just lay off the sweets between meals."

Barrett hesitated with the knife hanging over the pie. He didn't want to spend the season on the bench, and he knew his game would be better if he lost a little weight. He ran one hand over his belly. He had chubbed out over the winter, and he was slower on the field.

Barrett could smell the chocolate pie and his mouth watered. He wanted a piece of pie right now. He really, really wanted a piece.

But he could live without it. He could wait for dinner. Barrett pushed the pie away and laid down the knife. He picked up an apple instead and returned to his television program.

The chocolate pie tasted twice as good after dinner just because Barrett had waited. The next day at practice the coach told him he was getting faster.

Your Turn

Have you ever talked yourself into doing something you knew you shouldn't do? How did you feel about it later?

Prayer

God, sometimes I want to do things I shouldn't do. Make me strong and help me do the right thing. Amen.

PASSING THE TEST

Before Jesus started His ministry, he went away to pray alone about what following God meant to Him. While He was alone, He was tempted to disobey God. In Matthew 4:1-11 you can read about the temptations Jesus faced. Match each of the temptations listed below to the statement that best describes Jesus' reason for resisting the temptation.

1. Jesus was tempted to turn stones into bread.
2. Jesus was tempted to jump off a mountain and command angels to save Him.
3. Jesus was tempted to worship the devil and become ruler of the world.

A. Worshiping the one, true God is more important than power or money.
B. Obeying God is more important than showing off to impress other people.
C. Doing God's will is more important than physical comforts.

(The solution is on page 246.)

God wants me to be honest about what I believe.

If you tell others that you belong to me, I will tell my Father in heaven that you are my followers.

– Matthew 10:32 CEV

Holy Joe

Tim sat down next to Reed on the school bus.

"What a pile of books," Tim said. "You must have a lot of homework."

Tim looked more closely at Reed's books.

"Is that a Bible? Why are you carrying it? Are you a Holy Joe or something?"

Reed wondered what to say. He liked going to church, but he didn't want to be teased about it. Maybe he could pretend he was bringing his Bible to school for an assignment in World Lit.

That might work, but it would be a lie. Reed didn't feel right lying about his faith. That would be like pretending not to believe in Jesus.

"Yeah, I bring my Bible to school," Reed said. "Sometimes when I get my homework finished I have time to read my Bible in study hall."

"Why do you read the Bible?" Tim asked. "Isn't it boring?"

"Oh, no, the Bible has great stories in it!" Reed said. "There are battles and giants and all sorts of cool stuff."

Reed swallowed hard and took a deep breath.

"And there are stories about Jesus," he said. "Those are my favorites."

"I don't know anything about Jesus," Tim said. "My family doesn't go to church. I don't think we even have a Bible in my house."

"If you'd like to borrow my Bible sometime, I can show you where some of the good stories are," Reed offered.

Tim shrugged and stood up as the bus came to a stop.

"I don't know. Maybe," he said. "I get off here. See you later, Reed."

Tim had called him "Reed." No teasing! And Reed hadn't lied about his faith!

Reed settled back in his seat with relief and waved through the window to Tim.

Your Turn

Does it bother you to talk about what you believe? Why or why not?

____

____

Prayer

Jesus, I know You're proud to be my friend. I'm proud to be Your friend, too, and I want everybody to know it. Amen.

THE GREAT COMMISSION

Jesus told His disciples not to keep the good news of His resurrection a secret, but to share it with people everywhere they went. Matthew 28:19-20 is sometimes called "The Great Commission." Unscramble the phrases below to see what Jesus wants Christians to do. The solution is on page 246.

and go Therefore

____

disciples all of nations make

____

the in name Father of baptizing them the

____

Son the the Holy Spirit of of and and

____

obey them teaching to and

____

I you commanded have everything

____

Kindness is better than winning.

Anything you did for one of the least important of these brothers and sisters of mine, you did for me.

– Matthew 25:40 NIRV

Last-place Louie

Wally loved kickball and he loved winning. Today it was his turn to be a team captain. Wally and the other captain chose teams carefully, picking the best players first. Wally wanted to make his team as strong as possible.

Some of the kids waved their hands and pleaded, "Pick me! Pick me!"

But Louie stood off to one side, quietly scuffing the asphalt with one shoe. Louie was always the last to be chosen. He just wasn't any good at sports. If the ball came to him, he dropped it. When he ran bases, he always stumbled. And as for kicking, forget it.

Wally felt a little sorry for Louie. Wally also felt sorry for himself. He counted how many players were left to pick and saw that Louie was going to end up on his team. As he expected, the other captain chose Linda Jo and Louie was the last person waiting.

Wally was about to call Louie to join his team when Stuart came jogging from the school building. Stuart had been helping the teacher with a project, so he was late arriving on the playground. Wally's heart jumped! Stuart was great at every sport. With Stuart on his team, they'd win for sure.

Wally was all set to call Stuart's name when he saw the sad look on Louie's face. Somebody on Wally's team shouted, "Choose Stuart!" Somebody else yelled, "Yea! We didn't get stuck with Last-Place Louie."

Wally wondered how it felt to always be chosen last. He decided that maybe winning wasn't the most important thing after all. To everyone's surprise, Wally chose Louie to play for his side.

Wally's team got stomped, but he didn't feel bad. In fact, he felt good about himself. He'd rather be a good person than a good captain.

Your Turn

Do you know a "Last-Place Louie"? How do you treat him?

____

____

Prayer

Jesus, when I see people that get left out, help me treat them the way I would treat You. Amen.

WHO'S THE WINNER?

The winner isn't always the person who gets the first place prize. Sometimes it's the person who does his very best, plays honestly or shows respect to others. After you play this game with a friend, make a list of the people from the game board who are the REAL winners.

To play the game you'll need a coin and a board marker for each player. Flip the coin to decide how many spaces to move: one space for heads and two for tails. There are additional instructions on some of the spaces. If you play alone, keep count of how many turns it takes you to get all the way to the end and next time try to beat your best game. Enjoy! Who are the real winners?

MAKING
FRIENDS

GETTING ALONG

God wants me to do my best to get along with others.

If it is possible, as far as it depends on you, live at peace with everyone.

– Romans 12:18

Bugged

"That Joseph drives me crazy," Neal said.

Neal and Adam were shooting hoops. Neal paused and took a shot from the free-throw line. The ball hit the rim, bounced high and fell through the basket.

"Joseph thinks he knows more than everybody else," Neal went on. "No matter what you say, he tells you you're wrong. Doesn't that drive you nuts?"

Adam shrugged and said, "I don't let it get to me."

Adam took a shot. Neal jumped for the rebound and put the ball through the net again.

"Doesn't anything bug you?" Neal asked. "I've never heard you complain about anybody."

Adam did a perfect lay-up and bounced the ball back to Neal.

"What's the point in getting all bent out of shape?" Adam asked. "God put all kinds of people on earth, and I just try to get along with everybody."

Neal took a long hook shot and missed the backboard completely. He retrieved the ball and took another shot.

"But some people are just so annoying," Neal insisted.

"You can always find something you don't like about a person," Adam said, "but you should make the best of it. They can probably think of something they don't like about you, too."

"Not me," Neal grinned. "Everything about me is likeable."

"Yeah, you're the exception," Adam said, grinning back. "In fact, it really irritates me that you're so perfect."

"And it bugs me that you like everybody," Neal said. "But I'll get used to it."

"Let's play one-on-one," Adam said, "and you can get used to losing."

Your Turn

What can you do to get along with people who annoy you?

____

____

Prayer

God, help me remember that everybody else doesn't have to be just like me. Show me how to get along with people who are different. Amen.

DIFFERENT IS GOOD

Isn't it great that God made everyone different? The world would be a boring place if we all liked to do the same things, looked alike and were interested in the same things. Sometimes the key to getting along with another person is finding out how you are alike and how you are different. Put your name in one of the three triangles shown below, then write things about yourself in that triangle. Put the names of two of your friends in the other two triangles and write things about them that are different from you. In the space in the middle where the triangles come together, make a list of some of the ways you and your friends are the same.

The people I hang with will shape who I am.

Bad company corrupts good character.

– 1 Corinthians 15:33

Bad Company

"I'm going out for a while," Rich said, heading out the door.

"Are you going to Wayne's house?" Rich's mother asked.

Rich shrugged. "I might end up over there."

"We need to talk," Mrs. Corrigan said.

She sat on the front steps and Rich settled beside her.

"Have you noticed that Wayne keeps getting you in trouble?"

"That's not true," Rich said.

"No? Whose idea was it to put a cherry bomb in Mrs. Worthington's mailbox?"

"Wayne did that, not me," Rich said.

"But you were there, and you had to help pay for the mailbox. Remember? And then you were in trouble last week because of cheating on your math test."

"I told you I didn't cheat."

"I believe you, but the teacher saw Wayne copying answers from your paper and you both had to see the principal. Right?"

"Yeah," Rich said quietly.

"Let's see," Mrs. Corrigan said. "Then there were the broken bottles in the school parking lot. And the graffiti. And the prank phone calls. And the..."

"Okay!" Rich said. "Wayne likes to fool around, but I'm not doing that stuff!"

"Maybe not," Mrs. Corrigan said, "but sooner or later Wayne will get you into serious trouble. If you hang out with Wayne he will rub off on you."

At first Rich was angry, but his mom's concern drained away his anger.

"I guess you're right, Mom," Rich admitted. "When I'm with Wayne it's like I turn into somebody else. He talks me into all sorts of crazy stuff."

Rich stood up and dusted off his jeans.

"I think I'll go see if Jerry wants to hang out," Rich said.

Your Turn

Which qualities make a good friend?

____

____

Prayer

God, I know good friends will help me be a good person. Help me find the right people to hang with. Amen.

FRIENDLY FACTS

Your friends can really make a difference in your life. Good friends are good for you! You need to choose your friends carefully and for the right reasons. Seven characteristics of a good friend are hidden in the word maze below. Circle the words in the maze. The first one is done for you. Do your friends think you have these characteristics? The solution is on page 246.

T R U S T K I N D

W O R T H Y H E L

S F R I E P F U L

U N D L Y F U N D

P P O R T I V E E

R E S P E C T P E

F U L N D A B L E

GETTING ALONG

Working together makes things turn out better.

Get all the advice you can, and you will succeed; without it you will fail.

– Proverbs 15:22 TEV

The Lightning Bolt

Harper looked at his go-cart with disappointment. It was just a downhill coaster, but the racer hadn't turned out the way he had hoped. In his mind, the Lightning Bolt was going to be a beauty, but it turned out to be a rolling mess.

As Harper frowned at the racer, his father came into the garage.

"How's it going?" Mr. Summers asked. "Are you ready for NASCAR yet?"

Harper shook his head sadly.

"The front wheels will barely turn," he said, "and one of the rear wheels is wobbly. The steering pulls to the left and the seat is loose. I tried to paint lightning on the side, but it looks more like a lumpy banana."

"Didn't your friend Kenny build a go-cart?" Mr. Summers asked. "Why didn't you get him to help you with the wheels?"

"I don't know," Harper said. "I guess I wanted to do it by myself."

"Doing things on your own is fine," Mr. Summers, "but sometimes it makes sense to ask for help. God gives us friends and family so we can help each other."

"I wish I'd thought of that before I messed up my go-cart," Harper said.

"Who says it's too late?" asked Mr. Summers. "Let's bolt down that seat."

After the seat was tight, Harper said, "Maybe Kenny can come over Saturday and help me with the wheels."

"And Willy is taking art classes," Harper's father said. "I'll bet he could turn that banana into a lightning bolt."

"Great," Harper said and laughed. "I don't want anyone to see me driving a banana-mobile."

Your Turn

How do you learn to do new things?

____

____

Prayer

God, I like to do things on my own, but sometimes I can use a hand. Help me to know when to ask for help. Amen.

A LITTLE HELP FROM MY FRIENDS

Everyone needs a little help now and then. Read these Bible stories to discover how people were helped by others. Match the story to the picture that shows the kind of help the people received. Write the name of the person under the matching picture. The solution is on page 246.

Moses (Exodus 17:10-12)

Paul (Acts 9:15-19)

A paralyzed man (Mark 2:3-12)

Jesus (Mark 11:1-7)

Jesus' Disciples (John 21:4-6)

Ruth (Ruth 2:5-13)

GETTING ALONG

Sometimes I need to let others know how I feel.

If your brother sins against you, go and show him his fault, just between the two of you.

– Matthew 18:15

Better Late Than Never?

"I'm not mad at you," Carl said to his friend Ted. "But I need to tell you that I'm tired of waiting on you. You're always late."

"That's just how I am," Ted said. "Running late is my secret super-power."

"You can joke about it if you want," Carl said, "but I'm serious. Every time we get together I end up waiting 15 or 20 minutes for you to get here. Last week you were a half-hour late and we missed the first 10 minutes of the movie."

Ted began, "I can't help it…"

"That's silly," Carl said. "All you have to do is leave 15 minutes sooner."

"I don't see the big deal," Ted said. He was starting to sound angry.

"The big deal," Carl said calmly, "is that when you're late over and over it makes me feel like I don't matter. It feels like my time isn't important and you don't care if I'm twiddling my thumbs waiting for you to get here."

"That's not true," Ted said. "You're my friend."

"That's why I'm telling you how I feel," Carl said. "We're friends and I want us to stay friends."

"Are you saying we can't be friends if I keep being late?" Ted asked.

"Of course not," Carl said. "But if you really are my friend I think you'll try to stop doing something that hurts my feelings."

Ted frowned silently for a minute, then his face relaxed into a grin.

"I guess you're right," Ted said. "From now on I'll try not to keep you waiting, but I can't promise I won't slip up sometimes."

"And I can't promise I won't leave without you next time," Carl said.

"Fair enough," Ted said, smiling. "There's no reason both of us should miss the beginning of the movie."

Your Turn

Was it hard for Carl to tell Ted what was bothering him? Why or why not?

____

____

____

Prayer

God, help me to know when to make the best of things and when to speak up about what's bothering me. Amen.

SPEAKING UP

Sometimes you can just forgive people or make the best of the things that bug you, but at other times you need to speak up for yourself. How can you know when you should speak up? Here are some questions to help you decide:

- If I keep quiet will this get better on its own or will the same thing keep happening over and over again?
- Does this person know that he or she is doing something that bothers me?
- If the person knew, would he or she care?
- Will speaking up probably make things better or worse?

When you do decide to talk to someone about something he or she has done to hurt you, here are some tips.

- Talk to the person privately so he or she isn't publicly embarrassed. (If this doesn't work, you can see about getting a parent or another friend involved, but one-on-one is the place to start.)
- Don't get angry or say hateful things.
- Don't try to punish the other person with your words.
- Tell the other person about your own feelings as clearly as you can.
- Say plainly what you want the other person to do or to stop doing.

And the most important advice comes from Ephesians 4:15:

SPEAK THE TRUTH ___ ___   ___ ___ ___ ___ .
1 2 3 4 5 6

Fill in the blanks above with these letters:

1. The Roman Numeral for one.
2. The first letter of the second half of the alphabet.
3. This sounds like a Spanish word for "the."
4. This letter looks like a hula hoop.
5. The shape of a flock of flying geese.
6. One kind of mail.

(The solution is on page 246.)

SHARING

God likes for me to share with others.

And do not forget to do good and to share with others, for with such sacrifices God is pleased.

– Hebrews 13:16

Jumbo Popcorn

"This is going to be a great movie," Nick said as they waited in line for the tickets. "I love science fiction. Some day I want to be an astronaut."

"The special effects are supposed to be awesome," Evan said. "The aliens are all computer generated."

Nick bought his ticket first, then waited for his friend. He noticed that Evan counted the dollar bills carefully as he took them from his wallet.

As they walked past the concession stand in the lobby, Evan said, "That popcorn sure smells good."

"Let's get some," Nick said.

Evan reached for his wallet then dropped his hand.

"I'm not really hungry," Evan said. "I don't want anything, but you go ahead."

Evan's dad had been laid off from work for a few months. Money was probably tight at Evan's house, Nick realized. He hoped Evan's dad would get back to work soon.

Evan seldom talked about his dad's job, but Nick could tell he was worried. Evan had told him that his family had decided not to take a vacation this summer so they could save some money.

Nick studied the prices at the concession stand. Then he glanced at his friend.

"You get a lot more for the money if you buy the jumbo popcorn," Nick said. "But that's more than I can eat by myself. If I get the large size would you help me eat it?"

"Uh, sure," Evan said. "I guess so. Thanks."

"No problem," Nick said. "It's no fun eating popcorn by yourself. While I wait in line, go get us some good seats."

Your Turn

Do you think sharing makes things more fun? Why or why not?

____

____

Prayer

God, I don't have everything I want, but I have enough to share with others. Thanks for giving me so much. Amen.

ENOUGH TO GO AROUND

Sharing with others is one of the ways you can say "thank You" to God for all the things God gives you. Read the story and follow the directions to help the boys share their lunches.

Zach, Ian, Tyler and Luis were going on an all-day bike trip. They were going to meet at the park at 9:00 and head up a mountain path that Zach's dad had shown him. Everyone was supposed to bring his own water and sack lunch. When the boys stopped for lunch, Zach realized he had forgotten his lunch. The other boys decided to share their lunches so Zach would have some food, too.

Choose things from each of the three sack lunches that the boys could share with Zach. Write or draw these items in Zach's empty lunch bag.

God is pleased when I help others.

Give to the one who asks you, and do not turn away from the one who wants to borrow from you.

– Matthew 5:42

Better Than a Ball Glove

"Dad, can I talk to you?" Roger Harper asked.

"Sure," his father said, lowering the Sunday paper. "What's up?"

"I've saved $25 to buy a new baseball glove," Roger said.

"You're getting pretty close," Mr. Harper said. "The new glove costs $35, right?"

Roger nodded.

Mr. Harper said, "You've worked really hard to save that money."

"I know you've been helping me, Dad," Roger said. "You've let me do extra jobs around the house to make money. That's why I wanted to talk to you."

"Roger, are you going to ask to borrow the $10 you need?" Mr. Harper frowned. "I thought we agreed you'd wait until you had all the money."

"No, that's not it," Roger said. "I'm not sure I still want to buy the glove."

Mr. Harper looked at his son in surprise.

"I thought you had your heart set on that glove," he said.

"I did," Roger said, "but I think I want to use the money for something else."

"Like what?" Mr. Harper asked.

"Remember in church they talked about that family whose house burned down?" Roger asked. "One of the guys in that family is in one of my classes. I've been thinking how awful it would be if everything I have was gone. My old glove isn't in such bad shape. I was thinking I might give my $25 to help that family."

"All of it?" Mr. Harper asked.

"Yeah, if it would be okay with you."

"Roger," Mr. Harper said, "It would be more than okay. I've never been more proud of you than I am right now."

Your Turn

After Roger gave away his money, do you think he felt sad about his choice? Why or why not?

____

____

Prayer

Lord, teach me to be generous with others, just the way You're generous with me. Amen.

GIVE A LITTLE

Did you know a bad attitude takes all the fun out of sharing with others? Paul told the Christians in Corinth what the proper attitude is for generosity. Read the Bible verses listed below that tell stories of generosity. Fill in the word that fits the clue, then copy the circled letters into the spaces to complete Paul's advice. (Use the New International Version of the Bible.)

The woman put in two copper ◯ __ __ __ __ . (Luke 21:2)

The boy shared his two __ __ __ ◯ . (John 6:7-11)

A woman poured an expensive bottle of __ ◯ __ __ __ __ __ on Jesus' head. (Matthew 26:6-7)

To help a friend, Jesus made __ __ __ ◯

from __ __ __ __ ◯ . (John 2:7-11)

The disciples chose seven men to serve as deacons and make sure the widows got enough ◯ __ __ __ . (Acts 6:1-6)

When an earthquake opened the doors of the prison, the jailer took

__ __ ◯ __ and Silas to his home, washed their wounds, and

listened to their message about Jesus. (Acts 16:25-34)

The boy also shared his five barley ◯ __ __ __ __ __ . (John 6:7-11)

"God loves a __ __ __ __ __ __ __ __ giver."
(2 Corinthians 9:7)

(The solution is on page 246.)

Listening is one way to show that I care about others.

Everyone should be quick to listen, slow to speak and slow to become angry.

– James 1:19

Open Ears

"I brought the snacks for our study time," Gavin said. "My mom always says the brain needs good food to do good work."

"Great!" Josh said. "Let's see the goodies."

Gavin opened the bag and set two cans of root beer on the table.

Josh made a face.

"What's the matter?" Gavin asked. "You said to get root beer for you."

"No, I didn't," Josh said. "I told you to get me anything but root beer. I can't stand that stuff."

"Sorry about that, but wait until you bite into this candy," Gavin said, holding out two Peanut Paradise bars.

Josh frowned and shook his head.

"Gavin, we've been friends almost two years. Are you telling me you don't know that I'm allergic to peanuts?"

"How am I supposed to know if you keep it a big secret?" Gavin snapped.

"I've only told you about a hundred times. You never listen to anyth…"

"Yes, I do!" Gavin interrupted.

"There you go, talking instead of listening," Josh said. "Yesterday you asked what snacks I like. While I was telling you, you started talking about a movie."

Gavin's face turned red. He opened his mouth to argue, then stopped himself. His parents and teachers always complained that he never listened.

"Maybe you're right," Gavin admitted.

He made a silent promise to bring Josh a jumbo box of chocolate-covered raisins the next day. Real friends don't just talk to each other, he decided. They also listen to each other.

Your Turn

Some people listen and others just wait for their turn to talk. What's the difference?

____

____

Prayer

God, help me to remember to give my mouth a rest sometimes while my ears get a work-out. Amen.

WHAT DID YOU SAY?

Sometimes you might think you know what someone said, but you didn't really understand what he or she meant. Good communication involves saying what you mean, listening carefully and really hearing what the other person is saying. Look at the statements below and circle the explanation that best describes what the person really means to say. The answers you give may not be the same as someone else's answers.

1. "I've already seen that movie, but I'm not too tired for a game."
   a. I'd like to go to the movie with you.
   b. I'd rather play basketball than go see that movie again.
   c. I'll go to the movie if you buy my ticket.

2. " I guess Matt's not so bad."
   a. I think we should invite Matt to our party.
   b. Matt's okay at school, but I don't want to hang out with him.
   c. Let's play a trick on Matt.

3. "Why do I have to have my little brother tag along everywhere I go?"
   a. Having a little brother is no fun.
   b. I wish I had sisters.
   c. I'll still do things with my brother, but sometimes I want to do things just with my friends.

4. "I've got to have a remote-controlled car."
   a. All my friends have remote-controlled cars and I feel left out when they play with them.
   b. You are bad parents for not getting me something I need.
   c. I can make a lot of money racing a remote-controlled car.

Since God forgives my mistakes, I should forgive the mistakes of others.

Bear with each other and forgive whatever grievances you may have against one another. Forgive as the Lord forgave you.
– Colossians 3:13

The Invitation

Aaron sorted through the letters and bills as he walked back from the mailbox. One letter was addressed to him. He opened it eagerly and pulled out the card. It was an invitation to Carter's surprise birthday party.

Yeah, like he was going to that party!

Only a month before, Aaron had a birthday party and had invited Carter. Carter had promised he'd come to the party. Aaron spent the whole evening watching for Carter, but he never showed up.

The next day at church, Aaron asked Carter, "Where were you last night?"

"I was at the mall. Why?"

"You missed my party!" Aaron said.

"Oh, man," Carter said. "I forgot all about it. I'm really sorry, Aaron."

"That doesn't help much," Aaron said. "I thought we were friends, but a real friend wouldn't have blown off my birthday."

Carter apologized and brought a present to Aaron.

"I got plenty of presents at my party," Aaron said. "I don't need any more."

Aaron read the invitation again. It was a surprise party, so Carter's mom must have invited Aaron. He tore up the invitation and shoved it in his pocket.

Maybe he was being silly. He missed Carter. This party might be a way to patch things up. If Aaron showed up at the party, Carter would be so happy.

It still hurt that Carter had forgotten Aaron's party. But anybody could make a mistake. Aaron took the torn pieces out of his pocket and laid them on the porch. He slid them together and stared at the invitation. Should he go or not?

Your Turn

Think of a time when somebody forgave you for doing the wrong thing. How did it make you feel?

____

____

Prayer

God, You have forgiven me so many times. If You can forgive me, then I will try to forgive others, too. But it's not easy, so please help me. Amen.

FORGIVER OR FORGIVEN?

The story of Jacob and Esau is a story about two brothers. Their cheating and lies caused hatred and separation between them. It was many years before forgiveness was part of their story. Read the Bible verses and the statements below. If a statement is true for Jacob, put a "J" on the line beside it. If it is true for Esau, put an "E" on the line.

Genesis 27:1-29

1.______He stole his brother's blessing from their father.

Genesis 27:41

2.______He hated his brother and promised to kill him.

Genesis 27:42-45

3.______His mother sent him away to escape his brother's anger.

Genesis 33:1-2

4.______He feared what his brother would do even though they had not seen each other for many years.

Genesis 33:3

5.______He bowed before his brother.

Genesis 33:4

6.______When he saw his brother, he ran to meet, hug and kiss him. He did not choose to kill his brother as he had promised years before.

Genesis 33:11

7.______He gave his brother gifts in gratitude for his forgiveness.

(The solution is on page 246.)

I can treat others the way I want to be treated.

Do to others as you would have them do to you.

– Luke 6:31

Papers in the Wind

Owen and Vic were at the bus stop as Ellen trudged up the hill toward them. As usual, she carried a huge stack of books.

"Here comes Super-Brain," Vic said.

"Do you think she gets anything less than 100 on her papers?" Owen wondered.

"As many books as she carries around, she must have muscles like a lumberjack," Vic joked.

The school bus came around the corner, its gears grinding. Ellen heard the bus and started to trot up the hill. As she hurried, a book slid out of her grip. When she grabbed at it, all the other books fell into the street. Some flopped open when they landed and the wind scattered papers tucked in the pages.

Ellen began to grab her papers, but the wind whipped them in all directions.

Watching the papers tumble through the streets, Vic started laughing.

"Come on," Owen said. "We'd better give her a hand."

"Help Super-Brain?" Vic asked. "You've got to be kidding."

Owen ran down the hill and helped Ellen chase the runaway papers.

"Thanks so much," Ellen said when the papers were back in her grip.

"No problem," Owen said, and they got on the waiting bus.

Owen sat down next to Vic and his friend whispered, "Why did you do that?"

Owen shrugged.

"I watched her chasing papers and I thought about how I'd feel if that were me," Owen said. "If it happened to me, I'd want somebody to give me some help, so that's what I did."

Owen glanced at his friend and added, "It's called the golden rule, Vic. Maybe you ought to think about it. Next time you might be the one who needs some help."

Your Turn

Jesus taught the Golden Rule: to treat others the way we want to be treated ourselves. What would your school be like if everyone followed that rule?

____

____

Prayer

Lord, help me remember that other people have the same feelings I do. Amen.

TO FORGIVE OR NOT TO FORGIVE

Jesus told a parable about a person who didn't follow the Golden Rule. First, read the parable (from Matthew 18:23-34) to find out what happened to the man. Then, imagine how the story would be different if the man had followed the Golden Rule and treated others the way he wanted to be treated. Rewrite the ending of the parable in the space below to show the happier ending the story might have had.

One day a king called in all his officials to find out what they owed him. One official was brought in who owed the king 50 million silver coins, but he didn't have any money to pay back the debt. The king ordered the official, his wife and children to be sold into slavery to pay back the debt. The official begged the king for mercy and forgiveness and promised to pay back the money. The king felt sorry for the man and told him he could go free and didn't even have to pay back the money. Imagine how great the official felt! As the official was leaving, he met another man who owed him 100 silver coins. He grabbed the man and started choking him and demanded payment of the money he owed. The man begged for mercy and forgiveness and promised to pay back the money he owed.

Now write a happier ending for the story.

WATCHING MY WORDS

God wants me to be careful with my words.

For the Scriptures say, "If you want a happy life and good days, keep your tongue from speaking evil, and keep your lips from telling lies."
– 1 Peter 3:10 NLT

Taming the Tongue

"I didn't mean to hurt his feelings," Dylan McCoy said. "I was just joking."

"Well, it wasn't a joke to Sam," said Dylan's father. "His parents called and told me Sam's been crying. What happened?"

Dylan didn't want to look his father in the eye, so he stared at his own shoes. "Sam got a bad grade on a homework assignment," Dylan said.

"And?" his father asked.

"I sort of told him he was dumber than a doorknob," Dylan admitted. "But I didn't mean it!"

His father said, "Next time, think before you speak. Once the words come out of your mouth, you can't take them back."

"Yeah," Dylan agreed. "I wish I'd never said it. Sam's hurt, his parents are mad at me and I feel terrible, all because of a few dumb words."

"Words are powerful," said Mr. McCoy. "The things you say can do a lot of good or a lot of harm. Your tongue may be little, but it's probably the strongest muscle in the whole body."

"Can I call Sam, Dad?" asked Dylan. "I want to say I'm sorry."

"Those are strong words, too," Mr. McCoy said. "I'm sure you can make things right with Sam."

"I guess so," said Dylan. "But it would have been a lot simpler if I'd just kept my mouth shut in the first place."

Your Turn

Words can help or hurt. Make a list of good things you can do with your words.

____

____

Prayer

Talking is a wonderful gift, Lord. Help me use it the way You want. Amen.

WISE WORDS

Foolish words can start fights and hurt feelings, but wise words bless you and the people around you. Can you think of some wise words? Write them below. (We've given you a few to get you started.)

WATCHING MY WORDS

Grumbling makes things worse.

Do everything without complaining or arguing.
– Philippians 2:14

What an Awful World!

Zach returned to the dugout shaking his head in disgust.

"Don't worry about it," Diego said. "Everybody strikes out sometimes."

"Hey, it wasn't my fault," Zach said. "That's the worst pitcher I've ever seen. The umpire is even worse. Can you believe he called that last pitch a strike?"

Diego sighed quietly. Nothing ever suited Zach. Everybody else was always wrong, and Zach loved to complain about it.

"That bat I used is no good," Zach said. "I think it must be bent."

Diego had hit a double with that same bat in the last inning, but he didn't mention it.

"Our batting order is a mess," Zach said. "The coach doesn't have a clue."

Diego shrugged and said nothing. He remembered a conversation with his *abuela*, his grandma. In a gentle voice his grandma had said, "Grumbling only makes things worse, Diego. Smiling never hurt anyone. If the world is such a bad place, then do something to make it better. Any dummy can complain and criticize. And most dummies do."

"Even if I got a hit, I'd probably never make it around the bases," Zach said. "What a crummy field! The baselines are crooked and the ground is too rough."

"It's better than playing in the street," Diego said.

"Not much," Zach snorted.

"When the game's over," Diego said, "we can go to my house and borrow a lawnmower. Then we could go into the outfield and cut down some of those weeds. That would improve the field."

"Are you joking?" Zach asked. "It's too hot for that. Let somebody else do it. Hey, what are you smiling at?"

"I was just remembering something my grandma once told me," Diego said.

Your Turn

When you frown, how does it make you feel? What about when you smile?

____

____

Prayer

Lord, not everything is going to turn out the way I want today. Let me be happy about the good things and try to improve the bad things. Amen.

A DOWNER OR A DOER?

Some people would rather complain than do something about a problem. You can be a person who chooses to take action rather than just grumble and complain. Read the problem situations described below and create an action plan to change each situation.

Your parents don't want to raise your allowance, but you want more money.

Action Plan:____________________

____

____

You seldom get to watch TV on weeknights because you have too much homework.

Action Plan:____

____

Your friends want you to go to a baseball game on Saturday, but your parents expect you to help clean out the garage on Saturday.

Action Plan:____

____

You've lost your homework assignment for the weekend and your parents won't let you go out with your friends until your homework is finished.

Action Plan:____

____

You want to swap trading cards with a particular friend, but other people always get to him before you.

Action Plan:____

____

WATCHING MY WORDS

I don't have to talk about everything I know.

Disregarding another person's faults preserves love; telling about them separates close friends.

– Proverbs 17:9 NLT

The Sleepover Secret

"You told what happened Friday night, didn't you?" Kirby asked. His face was red and he looked angry.

"I don't know," Jack said. "I might have mentioned it to a couple of the guys."

"I can't believe this," Kirby said. "I can't believe you'd talk about that."

On Friday, Jack had spent the night at the home of his friend Kirby. Late at night, after the boys had gone to bed, Kirby's father had come home shouting and slamming doors. Jack had woken up and asked if anything was wrong. In a miserable voice, Kirby told him that his father had been out drinking again.

"Don't tell anybody about this, okay?" Kirby had asked. In the dark Jack wasn't sure, but he thought Kirby was crying.

But on Monday it made Jack feel big to tell about Kirby's dad. Jack had shared the secret with three people and asked them not to spread it around. Of course, they told others and soon all Kirby's friends knew about the problem. Now Kirby was angry and Jack knew he had made a mistake.

"I'm sorry," Jack said. "I didn't mean any harm. It's not your fault your dad gets drunk."

"No, but it's your fault everybody knows about it," Kirby said. "I thought we were friends."

"But I am your friend," Jack insisted. "I'll never tell any more of your secrets."

"That's right," Kirby said angrily, "because you'll never be in my house again, and I'll never let you know another secret of mine."

Kirby turned and walked away. Jack watched him go, wishing he hadn't talked behind his friend's back.

Your Turn

Is it hard for you to keep quiet about things you know about others? Why or why not?

____

____

Prayer

God, when friends trust me, I don't want to let them down. Keep me from saying things that will embarrass others. Amen.

THE SECRET TELLER

There were people who didn't like Jesus and wanted to do Him harm, but the disciples were supposed to be Jesus' friends. Jesus trusted His disciples, but one of the disciples gave away a secret and caused a terrible thing to happen. The disciple was named Judas. Fill in his story in the story map below. After reading each passage, write briefly in the box what Judas or others did.

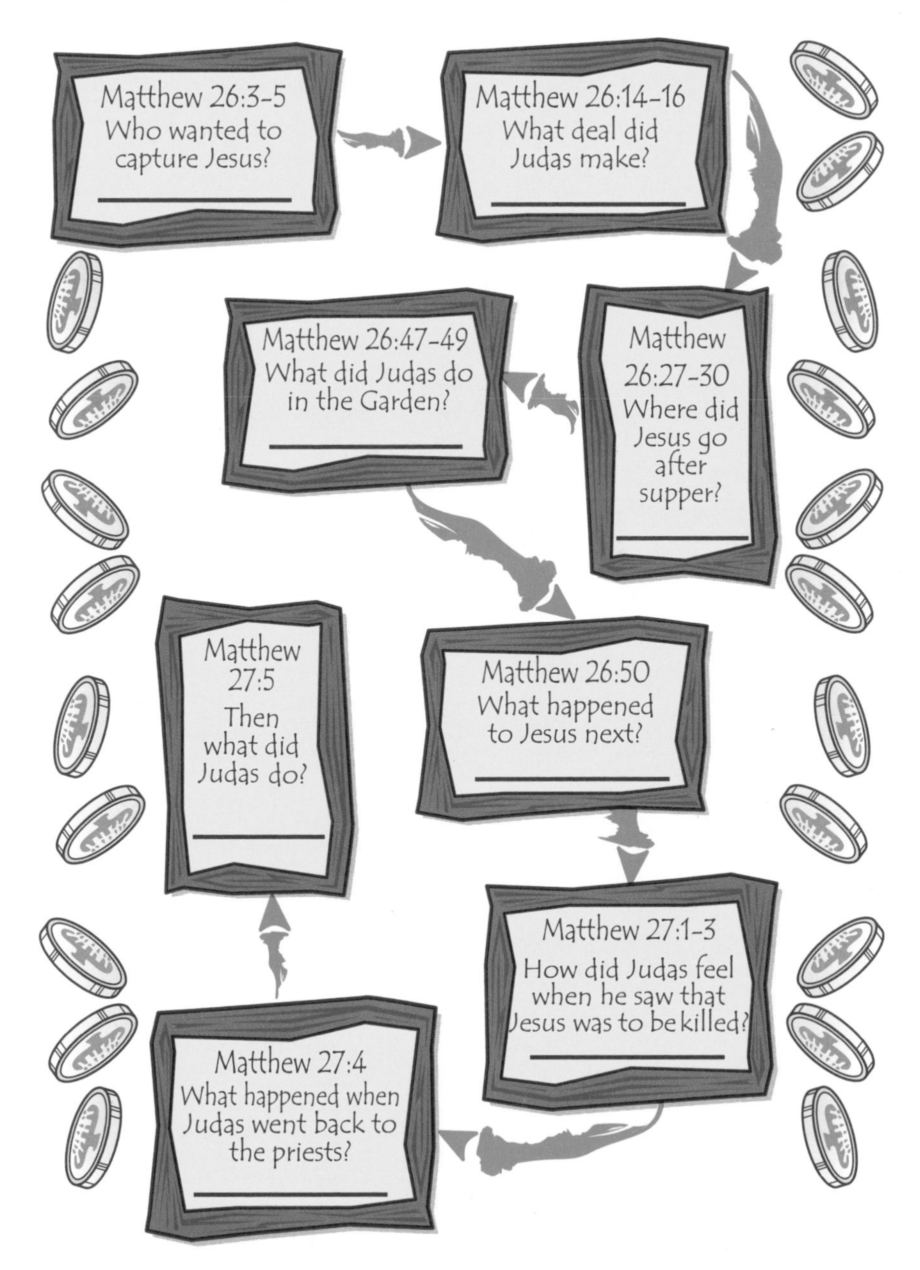

WATCHING MY WORDS

My words can make others feel better.

An anxious heart weighs a man down,
but a kind word cheers him up.

– Proverbs 12:25

Good Words on a Bad Day

"What a lousy day," Ned said. He stomped into the bedroom he shared with his brother, Paul. Ned threw his school books on the floor and fell on his bed.

Paul looked up from his homework and asked, "What's up?"

"Nothing is up," Ned moaned. "Everything is down. I barely passed my history test, the one I thought I was going to ace."

"How was practice?" Paul asked.

"Horrible," Ned said. "My batting was terrible. I did nothing but swing at air. If they'd thrown me a beach ball, I don't think I could have hit it."

"Even Babe Ruth was off sometimes," Paul said.

"And I had to make a speech in English today, but I left my notes at home. I worked hard on that speech, but I couldn't remember anything I was supposed to say. I bumbled around for five minutes and the whole class laughed at me."

Ned stared at the ceiling.

"My history teacher thinks I didn't study," he said. "The coach thinks I'm a loser, and my English class thinks I'm stupid. The whole world thinks I'm a dork."

"Not the whole world," Paul said. "I think you're the best brother in the universe."

"Yeah, right," Ned snorted.

"Hey, if you were stupid, you couldn't have helped me pass math last year," Paul said. "And I know you can bat, because you taught me."

Ned looked at Paul.

Paul said, "You're just having a bad day. But you're still my favorite brother!"

"I'm your only brother," Ned said.

"See?" Paul said. "You really are my favorite."

Ned sat up on his bed and smiled.

"Thanks, Squirt. Do you need any help with your math homework?"

Your Turn

Have you said something kind today? How can you plan to do so?

____

____

Prayer

God, give me the right words to make someone's day better. Amen.

I GET DOWN, YOU PICK ME UP

The things you say to people can make a big difference in their lives. If a person hears he is no good often enough, he begins to believe it. If a person is reminded that she is special, she feels good about who she is. Some things pick people up and other words can weigh them down. Read the words below. Draw a balloon around the pick-me-up words. Draw a brick around the drag-me-down words.

Get lost!

You were great!

Way to go!

Hey, loser!

Crybaby!

Nice job!

I am proud of you!

Great teamwork

Noodle-head!

WATCHING MY WORDS

I should build up others instead of tear them down.

Therefore encourage one another and build each other up.
– 1 Thessalonians 5:11

The Bowling Buddy

Eric lifted the bowling ball but as he went to roll it, he stumbled and dropped the ball. It bounced and crashed into the gutter. Eric watched it roll down the gutter, missing the pins completely. He wished he could turn invisible.

Eric slunk back to sit beside his friend Isaac who had invited him to go bowling.

"I haven't got the hang of it yet," Eric said, looking at the floor.

Isaac slapped him on the back and said, "You're doing great for your first time out. If you hadn't slipped you would have really nailed that one."

Eric looked at the score sheet and moaned.

"Don't worry about your score," Isaac said. "The main thing is to have fun."

"Everybody else is having fun," Eric said, "laughing at me."

"Nah!" Isaac said. "Nobody's paying any attention to you!"

Isaac stepped onto the floor and picked up his ball. He knocked down seven pins with his first bowl, and then picked off the other three on his second try.

When he came back to sit beside Eric, he said, "You should have seen me the first time I ever came bowling. I only got five pins all night!"

"I know the feeling," Eric said.

"Oh, you're a pro compared to me," Aaron said. "Twice I dropped the ball and it rolled back here into the seats. I thought I was going to die of embarrassment."

"You're kidding," Eric said.

"That wasn't the worst," Aaron said. "Once I bounced my ball into someone else's lane. Don't ask me how I did it."

Now Eric was laughing.

"That's how I got those five pins," Aaron admitted. "In somebody else's lane."

On Eric's next bowl he knocked over eight pins. Over the noise of the falling pins, he heard Aaron cheering for him.

Your Turn

Can you think of someone who needs encouragement? What could you say to help him or her?

____

____

Prayer

Lord, I want to be an encourager. Show me somebody I can build up. Amen.

BARNABAS, THE ENCOURAGER

In the book of Acts, we meet a fellow named Joseph who was always encouraging other people. Joseph was so kind and helpful that nobody called him by his real name. Instead, he was nicknamed Barnabas. In the language of those days, "Barnabas" meant "encourager."

Here are a few of the people to whom Barnabas gave encouragement. Read about the people and their problems. Then try to guess what you think Barnabas did to help. You can look up the stories to see if you guessed right.

1. Paul, a new Christian, came to Jerusalem to work with the church, but the other Christians were afraid of him and the church leaders avoided him. What do you think Barnabas did? (Acts 9:26-28)

____

____

2. In the city of Antioch, many people were becoming Christians. The church there needed help making those new Christians part of the family. What do you think Barnabas did? (Acts 11:19-26)

____

____

3. John Mark was a young Christian who had gotten halfway through a mission trip and quit. Now he wanted to join another mission trip, but Paul said he couldn't be trusted and refused to take him along. What do you think Barnabas did? (Acts 15:36-39)

____

____

(The solution is on page 246.)

MAKING GOD SMILE

FRUIT OF THE SPIRIT

God's Spirit is at work in me.

But the fruit of the Spirit is love, joy, peace, patience, kindness, goodness, faithfulness, gentleness and self-control.

– Galatians 5:22-23

Nine Ways to Make God Smile

Uncle Hal asked, "Remember the apple tree you helped plant a few years ago?"

"Yeah," said Price. "That was hard work."

"The hard work paid off," Uncle Hal said as he led Price to the tree.

"Wow!" Price said when he saw the tree full of shiny, red fruit.

Uncle Hal plucked an apple from the tree and pitched it to Price. Then he picked one for himself and bit into it. A huge smile spread across his face.

"Uncle Hal, you're really proud of this tree, aren't you?"

Price's uncle nodded happily.

"From all the other trees at the nursery, I picked this one," said Uncle Hal. "You and I dug the hole and staked the tree in place. I watered it and sprayed to keep the bugs away. Every summer I've looked for apples, and here they are!"

Price bit into his own juicy apple.

"When a tree bears fruit it means the tree is healthy," said Uncle Hal. "This tree is doing what God meant for it to do. It's no different for people."

"People don't bear fruit," Price said.

"Christians do," Uncle Hal said. "God's Spirit loves us and helps us grow, and after a while fruit starts to grow in our lives."

Price imagined himself planted with apples hanging from his fingers.

Uncle Hal laughed and said, "I know what you're thinking. The fruit of God's Spirit isn't apples. The fruit God looks for is love, joy and kindness."

"Is God proud of us when we bear fruit?" Price asked.

"Absolutely," Uncle Hal said, taking another bite of his apple. "There's a big smile on God's face every time a new fruit grows in your life."

Your Turn

Read the list of Spirit fruits at the top of the page. Which fruits are growing in your life right now?

____

____

Prayer

God, fill my life with the fruit of Your Spirit so the world can see that You are working in me. Amen.

Paul writes to his Galatian friends about nine different fruits of God's Spirit. Here is a list of those fruits, but the words are jumbled. Unscramble each fruit and write it on the tree. See if you can do all nine without looking back at the story!

FNLOE-RSOLTC
LETNENESGS
OJY
NIACTEEP
STFNHFEIUSLA
VELO
SKENDINS
ACEPE
DONSESOG

(The solution is on page 247.)

Love means caring about what others want.

Love one another.

– John 13:34

Burger Battle

"School's out," Mrs. Logan said. "Let's celebrate!"

"I want to go to Pancake Kitchen!" Maggie said.

"Yuck!" shouted Price. "They ought to call it Krummy Kitchen. Let's go to Burger Barn!"

"Pancake Kitchen has chocolate-chip waffles," Maggie said.

"Burger Barn has a playland," Price said. "And with the super-large cheesy fries you get a free toy."

"I want chocolate-chip waffles with marshmallow syrup," Maggie said in a small voice.

"If I can't go to Burger Barn…"

"Stop it!" Mrs. Logan said, holding up one hand. "You have five minutes to work this out in a loving way, or we'll eat leftovers tonight."

Mrs. Logan said "loving" extra loud and walked out of the room. Price wondered what love had to do with eating out. Then he remembered something he'd heard in Sunday school: Love doesn't insist on getting its own way.

"The last time we ate out, we went to Burger Barn, didn't we?" Price asked.

"Yeah," Maggie said, "and the time before that."

"Then I guess it's your turn to pick where we eat, Maggie," Price said.

Maggie gave him a hug and ran after her mother shouting, "We're going to Pancake Kitchen!"

Price felt good about giving in. Uncle Hal had told him that love is one of the fruits of God's Spirit. When we love each other it shows that God is at work in us. Uncle Hal said that every time the fruit of the Spirit grows in our lives, God smiles in gladness. The thought of God smiling made Price smile, too.

Your Turn

Write the name of someone you love. When was the last time you showed your love for that person? How could you do that today?

____

____

Prayer

Lord, love isn't just something I should say; love is something I should do. Help me show the fruit of love in my life today. Amen.

LOVE OR NOT

Love shows itself in the way you act and how you treat others. Here is a list of the way people act sometimes. Some things on the list are loving, and some are not. Draw a line connecting the things from the list to the correct phrase on the left. (If you need help, take a look at 1 Corinthians 13.)

Love Is...

Love Is Not...

patient
dishonest
grudging
kind
trusting
envious
rude
humble
boastful
selfish
generous
protective
hopeful
forever

JOY (FRUIT 2)

Jesus always brings joy.

Rejoice in the Lord always. I will say it again: Rejoice!
– Philippians 4:4

Pumpkin Pie and Joy

Price stooped, reached into the back of the cabinet and pulled out a can of pumpkin.

"Thank you, Price," Granny said. "My knees would hurt all day if I had to get down there."

She handed Price a can opener.

"My fingers aren't in such great shape, either," she said with a chuckle.

As Price opened the can he asked, "How can you laugh when you're hurting?"

Granny shrugged and spooned the pumpkin into a bowl.

"Life has good and bad," she said. "I learned a long time ago to keep my eyes on the good stuff."

"Like what?" Price asked.

"Like pumpkin pie and visits from my grandson," Granny said. "Flowers in the yard. Good friends. And even if I lost all of that, I'd still have Jesus."

Granny added spices and brown sugar to the pumpkin.

"Jesus is my best friend," Granny said. "If I get sad, it never lasts long. I just think about everything Jesus has done for me and how much He loves me."

She poured the pumpkin into two pans and slid them into the oven.

"Why did you make two pies, Granny?"

"One for us," she said, "and one for my neighbor. I like giving presents!"

So does Jesus, Price thought. Jesus had given Granny the gift of joy. She probably had other fruits of the Spirit, too, but joy filled her life the way the smell of pumpkin pie filled her kitchen. Just being around Granny made Price feel good.

"What are you grinning about?" Granny asked.

Price said, "I was just thinking that whenever I visit you I get pumpkin pie in my belly and joy in my heart."

Your Turn

Does buying things give you true joy. Why or why not?

____

____

Prayer

God, give me Your joy and show me how to share it with others. Amen.

REJOICE ALWAYS!

God's gift of joy will help you handle the hard things in life. If you can decode the message from Nehemiah 8:10, you'll get a happy reminder of how God's joy blesses you!

KEY

A = Z	B = Y	C = X	D = W	E = V	
F = U	G = T	H = S	I = R	J = Q	
K = P	L = O	M = N	N = M	O = L	
P = K	Q = J	R = I	S = H	T = G	
U = F	V = E	W = D	X = C	Y = B	Z = A

GSV QLB LU GSV OLIW

____

RH BLFI HGIVMTGS.

____

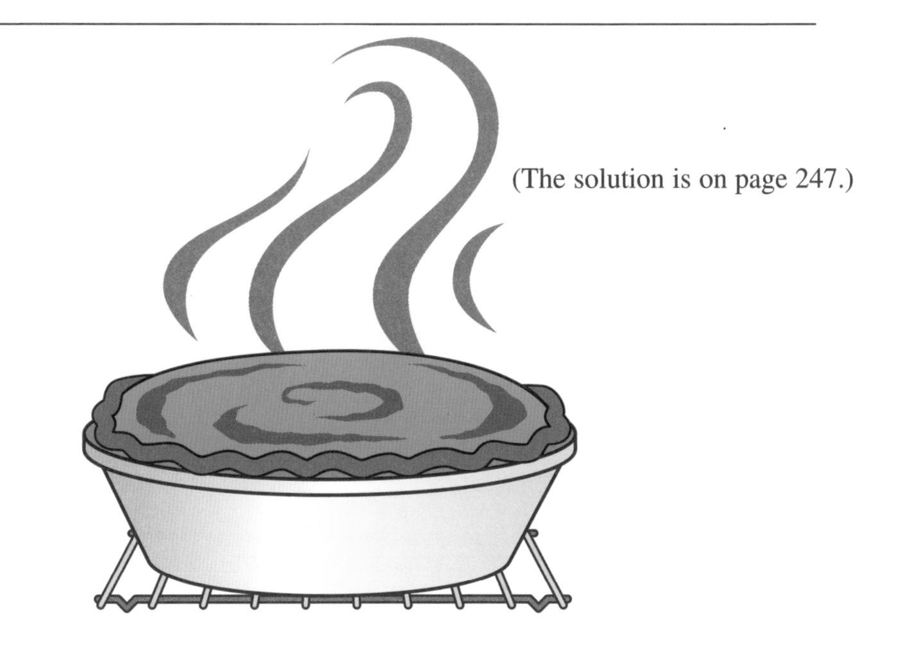

(The solution is on page 247.)

PEACE (FRUIT 3)

Peace is knowing that Jesus takes care of you.

Let the peace of Christ rule in your hearts.

– Colossians 3:15

The Storm Party

Ba-THOOOOM! The thunder roared so loudly that the house shook. A moment later the lights went out.

"Mommy!" squealed Maggie. "Why is it dark?"

"Don't be afraid," Mrs. Logan said. "The storm has blown down the power lines somewhere."

"I'll get a flashlight," Price said.

"I'm scared," Maggie whined.

"Scared of a little storm?" asked Mrs. Logan. "We four are going to be fine."

"Four?" asked Price.

"Sure," his mother said. "You, Maggie, me and Jesus."

"Hey, that's right," Price said. "Jesus is right here in the house with us, and He'll take care of us."

The thunder boomed again.

"Take Maggie downstairs," Mrs. Logan said. "I'll be down in a minute and we'll have a storm party."

Maggie sat up straight on the couch.

"That sounds like fun!" she said.

As Price led Maggie downstairs, Maggie asked, "Will we be okay?"

"Of course," Price said. "Jesus really is here. If you trust Him, He'll put peace in your heart and you won't be afraid."

A moment later Mrs. Logan joined them. She set down a lit candle and they sat around it. She handed both kids a skewer and then opened a bag of marshmallows.

"Have you ever roasted marshmallows over a candle?" she asked.

"Wow!" Maggie shouted. "I get to go first."

While they roasted marshmallows in the basement, the storm died down. The four of them had a fine party, and nobody was afraid.

Your Turn

When your thoughts are filled with Jesus, how do you feel?

____

____

Prayer

Jesus, thanks for taking away my worries and giving me Your peace. Amen.

PEACE RULES!

In the Bible there is a royal name given to Jesus that can remind you to not be afraid. Can you figure it out? Write the name in the spaces.

To figure out the message, mark out every B, S, L and W.
Change every Q into an E.
Change every X into a P.

X L B S W R I L B W N L S C Q

S B O B L S W F L S L W

X B L S Q W A L S B L W C S Q

___ ___ ___ ___ ___ ___   ___ ___

___ ___ ___ ___ ___

(The solution is on page 247.)

God wants me to be patient when people don't do things the way I think they should.

Be patient with everyone.

– 1 Thessalonians 5:14

Knot Patient

Price's little sister Maggie came into his room carrying a shoe in her hand. The laces were tangled in knots.

"Can you show me again how to tie my shoes?" Maggie asked.

Price closed the history book he was studying and looked at Maggie. A dozen mean answers flashed through his head.

He could have said, "I've already shown you 287 times."

Or he might have said, "Give it up! Just tape your shoes on your feet."

But Price reminded himself that patience is one of the fruits God likes to see in our lives and he said, "Let's see if I can get the knots out."

Price untangled the knotted laces.

"Okay, put this on your foot and let's try it again."

Price put one foot next to Maggie's and untied his own shoe.

"We'll go slowly," he said. "I'll tie my shoe and you tie yours. Do it as I do."

Price tied an overhand knot and Maggie did the same. Then he gathered one lace in a loop and wrapped the other lace around it. Maggie did the same with her chubby fingers.

"Now push that part through and pull it tight," Price said, leading the way.

Maggie squealed with delight.

"It worked! I tied it," she said. "I'll never have to ask for help again."

"Sure," Price said.

Ten minutes later Maggie returned to his room. Her shoes were on her feet, but the laces of both were untied and dragging on the floor.

"I think I forgot again," she said.

Price laughed and laid down his book.

Your Turn

When is it hard for you to be patient?

___

___

Prayer

God, You're always patient with me, so I'm going to try to be patient with others. Amen.

How patient are you? Can you find the word PATIENT in this word search? The word is hidden 10 times! Are you patient enough to find them all?

Q O X N D P V I E N P H
T N E I T A P S M D A E
D T N E I T A P K T T N
T H D I O I N V N W I N
N H D H U E M E N G E T
E N X C O N I E R Y N N
I H G A I T T Y E F T E
T F D H A N Z I H E N I
A H A P A T I E N T Q T
P A T I E N T F H I H A
I V R B Z P I E R M A P
P T N E I T A P H F S K

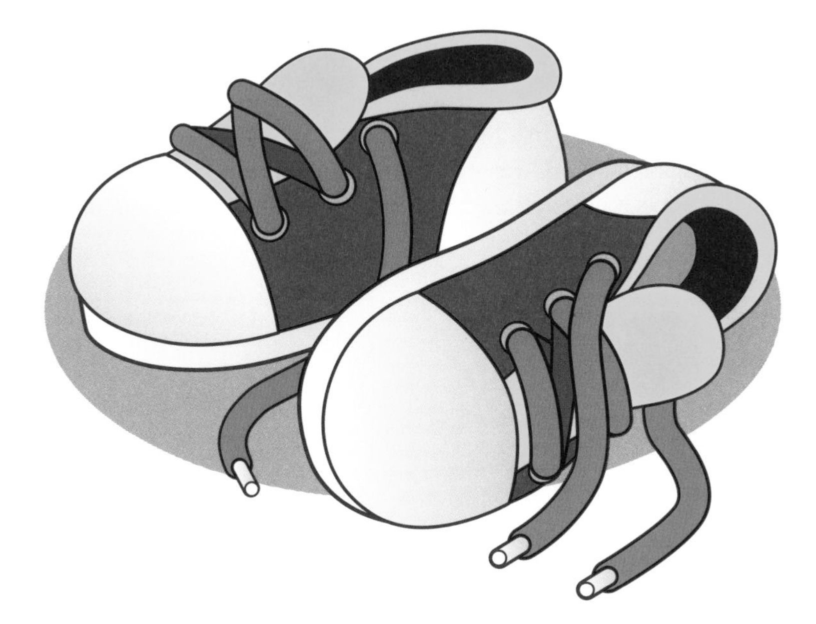

(The solution is on page 247.)

KINDNESS (FRUIT 5)

Kindness is doing nice things for others.

Be kind and compassionate to one another.

– Ephesians 4:32

Wet and Late

"Mom, I'm home!" Price Logan called.

"Don't take another step, young man!" his mother said. "You are soaked to the skin and you're dripping on my clean floor."

Mrs. Logan brought a towel. She scowled at Price as he dried himself.

Price's little sister, Maggie, joined them at the back door.

"You're wetter than a goldfish," Maggie said.

"And you're late for dinner," Mrs. Logan told him.

"I'm sorry, Mom," Price said. "I was on my way home when I saw Mrs. Curry in her front yard trying to get her lawnmower started."

Mrs. Curry was an elderly neighbor whose husband had died recently.

"Her grass was almost up to my knees," Price said, toweling his damp hair. "So I got her mower started and mowed her lawn."

"Did you finish before the rain started?" Mrs. Logan asked.

"Just in time," Price said. He grinned. "But then I had to ride my bike home in the storm."

Mrs. Logan smiled at her son.

"Price, I'm very proud of you," Mrs. Logan said. "I'll heat up your supper."

As Price came from his room wearing dry clothes, he heard Maggie ask, "Why did Price cut that lady's grass?"

His mother answered, "Because Price is kind."

Kindness, Price remembered, was one of the fruits of the Spirit that Uncle Hal had told him. Price sat down at the table and his mother set a plate in front of him.

"Are you cold?" Mrs. Logan asked.

"No, I feel great," Price said. "Just great!"

Your Turn

Have you been kind to anyone this week? How?

____

____

Prayer

God, help me notice today the people who need some kindness. Amen.

RANDOM ACTS OF KINDNESS

Sometimes you might miss chances to be kind just because you're not paying attention. In the space below, write the names of five people you expect to see this week. Beside each name write one kind thing you might do for that person. Now circle one kind deed that you are willing to do today.

Goodness is living like Jesus.

Anyone who does what is good is from God.
– 3 John 11

Treasure in a Trash Bag

Price leaped for the football, but it sailed overhead just beyond the reach of his fingers. The ball bounced crookedly into thick bushes. Price and his friend Tomas were enjoying the day in the city park, passing the football in a grassy field.

Price pushed through the green branches and picked up the football. Then he noticed a spilled garbage bag in the bushes. A coin on the ground caught his eye.

"Hey, Tomas," he yelled. "Take a look at this."

"Wow! That's a gold coin," Tomas said.

Price peered into the trash bag. He saw a few old coins, but mostly empty coin wrappers and containers.

"This is somebody's coin collection," Price said, "or what's left of it."

"What's it doing here?" Tomas asked.

"I think this stuff is stolen," Price said slowly. "Somebody stole all this, shoved it in the bag and brought it here to sort through it."

"Why'd they leave the gold coin behind?"

"Maybe it was dark and they missed it," Price said.

"Man, you have all the luck," Tomas complained. "I bet that gold coin is worth a hundred bucks."

"I'm not going to keep it," Price said in surprise. "I'm going to call the police. There's not much left here, but maybe they can get it back to the people it belongs to."

A few days later the owner of the coin collection phoned Price.

"I'm glad to get the gold coin back," he told Price. "That was a gift from my grandfather and it means a lot to me. Thanks for doing such a good thing. The world would be a better place if people would just be good to each other."

Your Turn

Do you ever ask yourself, "If Jesus were in my place, what would He do?" Why or why not?

___

___

Prayer

God, I want to be more like Jesus. Show me some good things I can do today. Amen.

FOR GOODNESS SAKE

The Bible says that Jesus went around doing good (Acts 10:38). Do you know the kinds of things Jesus did? A few are listed below. Draw each good deed the way you imagine it might have looked. (If you want to find out more, you can look up the stories in your Bible.)

Jesus fed a hungry crowd. (Matthew 14:15-21)	Jesus raised a little girl from the dead. (Matthew 9:18-26)
When the disciples were in a boat, Jesus stopped a storm that was scaring them. (Matthew 8:23-26)	Jesus gave sight to blind people. (John 9:1-7)

FAITHFULNESS (FRUIT 7)

Faithfulness means hanging in there.

I have fought the good fight, I have finished the race, and I have kept the faith.

– 2 Timothy 4:7

The Boring Meeting

"I don't want to go the youth group meeting tonight," Price Logan said. "Our meetings are so boring. We do the same thing every week. We eat dinner – always hot dogs and chips. We have a Bible study. Then we play volleyball."

"I guess that does get boring," his mother agreed.

"A lot of the kids have stopped going," Price told her.

"That's a shame," she said. "But you've got new leaders, right? Didn't the Conners start a couple of weeks ago?"

"Yeah, and they're real nice," Price said. "But the meetings are still boring."

"Maybe you should talk to them about doing some new things," Mrs. Logan said.

Price shrugged.

"I don't know," he said.

"I'll bet the Conners are counting on faithful members like you to help the youth group get a fresh start," Mrs. Logan said. "The Conners are making a commitment to you kids. Are you willing to make a commitment to them?"

Price had been thinking a lot lately about the fruits of God's Spirit. He knew faithfulness was one of the fruits God looks for in a Christian's life, but he hadn't been able to figure out what faithfulness meant. Maybe this was it. Maybe faithfulness is keeping a commitment even when you want to quit.

"Okay," Price said. "I guess we ought to give the Conners a fair chance. Will you drive me to church?"

"Sure," Mrs. Logan said. "Tell the Conners I'll fix dinner for the youth group next week. And I promise no hot dogs!"

Your Turn

Faithfulness means not being a quitter. Can you think of areas in your life where faithfulness is very important?

____

____

Prayer

God, You never give up on me. Thanks for Your faithfulness! Amen.

HANGING TOUGH

Paul, the apostle, understood the importance of faithfulness. He hung in there even when things got tough, and sometimes things got very tough for Paul. Fill in the crossword squares with these hardships that tested Paul's faithfulness to Jesus.

shipwrecks	flogging	whipping	stoning
bandits	enemies	prison	hunger
thirst	danger	riots	

(The solution is on page 247.)

Gentleness means being tender with others' feelings.

Let your gentleness be evident to all.

– Philippians 4:5

The Splinter

"Let's take a look at that splinter," Price said to his little sister.

Maggie extended one finger. The splinter was buried under Maggie's skin.

"We have to get that out," Price said.

His sister jerked her hand back.

"No!" Maggie yelled.

"If it hurts too much, you tell me and I'll stop, okay?" asked Price. "But first I'll show you my super-secret way of keeping splinters from hurting."

He went into the house and returned with a needle and an ice cube.

"Hold this ice cube on the splinter," Price said. "The cold will keep your finger from hurting."

After a few minutes Price took the ice cube and dropped it in the grass. He held his sister's finger firmly with one hand and the needle in the other hand.

"As soon as it hurts too much, you tell me," Price said. "Don't watch. Look at that dog across the street and tell me what he's doing."

"He's trying to sneak up on a squirrel," Maggie said. "The squirrel is watching the dog. Now he's going up a tree. The dog is barking and…ouch!"

"I'm finished," Price said. On one fingertip he held out the splinter for Maggie to see.

"That's a big one!" she said. "But it didn't hurt much when you took it out. Only a little at the end. You're very…I can't think of the word. You're very…"

"Gentle?" said Price.

"Yeah, gentle," Maggie said.

"When God sees gentleness in us, it makes God smile," Price said.

"Then God must be smiling at you right now," Maggie said, throwing her arms around Price's neck. "And so am I."

Your Turn

Write the names of three people you know who are gentle with you.

____

____

Prayer

God, thanks for being gentle with me! Help me remember to be gentle with others, especially the ones who are smaller than me. Amen.

CUT AND PASTE

Don't you wish you could cut and paste your talk the way you cut and paste over mistakes on a computer? Here are some words that need cutting and pasting. Figure out a gentle answer in each of these situations and write it in.

SELF-CONTROL (FRUIT 9)

God helps me make good decisions even when I'm scared or upset.

For God did not give us a spirit of timidity, but a spirit of power, of love and of self-discipline.

– 2 Timothy 1:7

Almost Batty

Price Logan was visiting his Uncle Hal. They were in his uncle's big back yard looking at the apple tree as the sun went down.

"The last time I was here," Price said, "you told me about the fruit of the Spirit."

"When God's Spirit comes into our lives, good things start growing," Uncle Hal said. "Things like love, joy and peace."

"And patience, kindness, goodness and faithfulness," Price said, grinning.

"Somebody's been reading his Bible," Uncle Hal said.

Something flitted through the darkening air.

"Was that a bird?" Price asked.

"No," Uncle Hal said. "The bats are coming out."

"Bats?" Price asked. His eyes got big. "Do they bite?"

"They won't bother us," Uncle Hal said. "They're hunting for moths and mosquitoes. Do they scare you?"

"A little bit," Price admitted.

"Then we'll go inside," Uncle Hal said.

Once they were in the house, Price felt better.

"I almost ran for cover," Price said.

"I'm glad you kept calm," Uncle Hal said. "The bats aren't dangerous, but running through the dark is. You might have stepped in a hole."

Uncle Hal pretended to pluck something from his nephew's ear.

"What's this?" he asked. "It looks like the fruit of self-control."

Price laughed.

"You never know when the fruit might show up, huh?" asked Uncle Hal.

Your Turn

Do you sometimes do things you later wish you hadn't done? Like what?

____

____

Prayer

God, help me control myself when I'm scared or angry or impatient. Thanks! Amen.

GETTING A GRIP

Everyone needs help with self-control sometimes. Circle the areas where you would like to have more self-control in your life (or write your own ideas on the blanks).

SPENDING

GETTING ANGRY

GETTING SCARED

SAYING DUMB THINGS

____

TELLING LIES

EATING TOO MUCH

______________________ The next time you find yourself doing something for which you'll be sorry, try out the **Four Secrets of Self-Control:**

✓ **Stop and think first!** Ask yourself if this is really what you want to do. How will it turn out? How will you feel about it tomorrow?

✓ **Plan ahead!** Before you get into hard situations, figure out ahead of time how you want to handle them. Make a plan and stick to it.

✓ **Ask God for help!** Say a quick prayer when you have trouble. Ask God to help you to decide and to do the right thing.

✓ **Don't give up!** It takes time to change the way you think and act. But you really can change if you keep trying and asking for God's help.

HANDLING THE HARD STUFF

HARD STUFF WITH OTHERS

I shouldn't believe everything I hear.

Dear friends, do not believe every spirit, but test the spirits to see whether they are from God.

– 1 John 4:1

Cabbage and Coconut

"I can't believe I flunked that biology test," Foster said to his friend Hiroshi as they walked home from school. "What did you get?"

"It was a tough test," Hiroshi agreed. "I got a B."

"I don't get it," Foster moaned. "I did everything to get ready. I ate cabbage every night last week."

"Cabbage?"

"Yeah, a woman on TV said cabbage improves your memory," Foster explained. "And I switched to coconut shampoo. The smell is supposed to make your brain work better."

"Uh-huh," Hiroshi said, holding his nose. "I noticed."

"The night before the test I slept with my feet propped up to make more blood run to my head. Somebody told me that helps your brain, too."

"I'll bet that was uncomfortable," Hiroshi said.

"I even slept with my biology book under my pillow," Foster said. "A guy on the radio said that the information will soak into your head if you do that."

Foster kicked at a rock on the sidewalk.

"See? I did everything to get ready for that test," he insisted.

"Did you study?" Hiroshi asked.

"Not exactly," Foster said. "I didn't think I needed to study."

"Foster, you've got to stop listening to all the goofy stuff people tell you," Hiroshi said. "Get a clue, buddy. You can't believe everything you hear."

"I guess you're right," Foster said. "I'd better check things out from now on and be more careful about what I believe."

Your Turn

Do you think advertisers say things that aren't true? Why would they do that?

____

____

Prayer

God, make me smart enough to ask questions and to know that some people don't tell the truth. Amen.

THE WHOLE TRUTH AND NOTHING BUT THE TRUTH

You're too smart to believe everything you hear and read, but is there anything you can count on? Sure, there is! Fill in each blank with one letter and you'll discover something you can always believe. The solution is on page 248.

Something to put a golf ball on ____

A letter that looks like a goal post ____

Something to yell on a roller coaster ____

A letter that looks like two mountains upside down ____

A letter that looks like a doughnut ____

A letter that rhymes with "star" ____

A letter that looks like half a pizza ____

A letter you could wear on your finger ____

Rhymes with "deaf" ____

A letter that astronauts use to measure gravity ____

A letter that looks like zero ____

Another half pizza ____

HARD STUFF WITH OTHERS

Trying to get even only makes things worse.

Do not repay anyone evil for evil.

– Romans 12:17

Getting Even

Ollie went over to where Vince was sitting in their school cafeteria.

"I know what you did," Ollie said. "You're the one who squirted epoxy glue into my bicycle lock."

Everybody at Vince's table laughed again.

"Yeah, it's real funny," Ollie said. "I had to leave my bike at school and walk all the way home yesterday. Then I delivered newspapers on foot, and after dinner my dad brought me back here and I had to cut the lock off my bike."

Vince leaned back in his chair.

"So I've been thinking about the best way to pay you back," Ollie said. "I guess I could do something mean to you. And then you'd do something mean to me again, only bigger."

"Sounds like fun," Vince said.

"Not really," Ollie said. "So I thought I'd try something different."

Ollie dropped a piece of paper onto Vince's tray.

"It's a ticket to a rock concert at my church this Saturday night," Ollie said. "The band is pretty good. You like rock music, don't you?"

"Uh, yeah," Vince said.

"Great! My dad and I will pick you up around 7:00. Okay?"

"Sure," Vince said. "Sounds good to me."

Vince looked at the ticket and back at Ollie.

"About the bike lock," Vince said. "I didn't mean to cause you so much trouble. I guess I wasn't thinking."

"No problem," Ollie said. "See you Saturday."

Your Turn

What would have happened if Ollie had tried to get revenge on Vince?

____

____

Prayer

God, it's not easy, but I know making peace is better than getting even. Teach me new ways to love the people who do me wrong. Amen.

PEACEMAKERS ARE WINNERS

God teaches a special way of settling up with those who have done you wrong. The secret is hidden in the letter maze. Begin with the circled letter and follow the message letter by letter all the way to the period. Your line will twist and turn! Work carefully and you'll find a message from Romans 12:21. The first two letters are done to get you started. Get going!

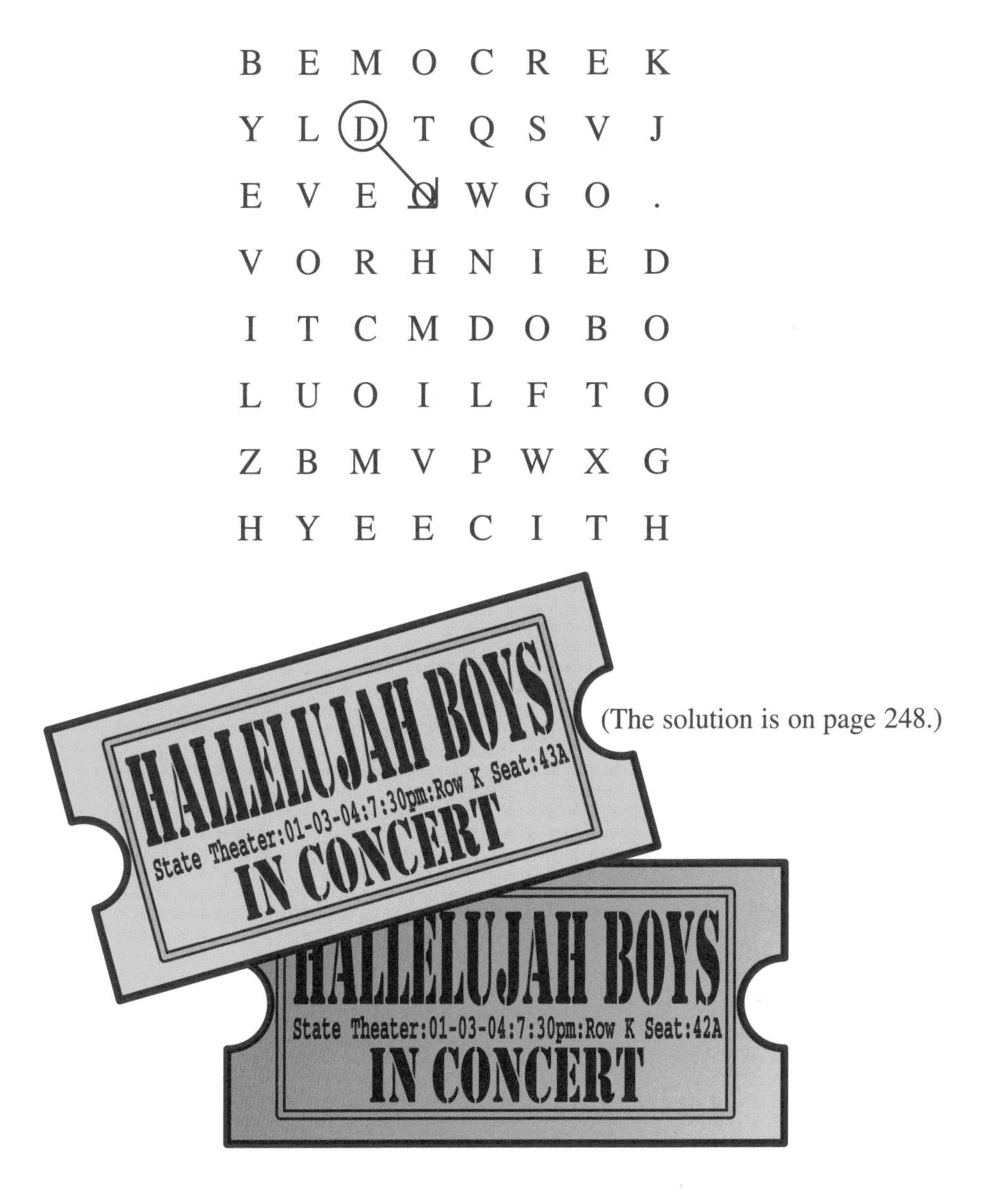

(The solution is on page 248.)

HARD STUFF WITH OTHERS

God wants me to honor what is mine and what is not.

You shall not steal.

– Exodus 20:15

Turning the Tables

Danny grinned at his buddy Chris as they came out of the drugstore. He reached into his coat pocket and pulled out two chocolate bars.

"How about a snack?" Danny asked.

"I didn't see you pay for those," Chris said.

"Five finger discount," Danny said with a wink.

"You stole them?" Chris asked.

"Nah. They sort of fell into my pocket," Danny said. "Cool off."

"But they're not yours!" Chris said.

"They are now," Danny said. He started to unwrap one of the candy bars and then his eyes went wide.

"Hey! Where's my skateboard?" he said. "I left it propped against the building right there. It's gone!"

Danny ran up and down the sidewalk looking in every direction.

"Some stinking thief stole my board!" he shouted. "I can't believe it!"

"Cool off," Chris said. "Maybe it just sort of fell into somebody's pocket."

"It's my skateboard!" Danny yelled.

"Not any more," Chris said. "I guess the five finger discount isn't so cool."

"This is different," Danny said.

"No, it's not," Chris said. "Whether it's a candy bar or a skateboard, whether you rip off a person or a store, stealing is still stealing."

"I saved a long time to buy that board," Danny said.

"I'll help you look for your skateboard," Chris said, "but I hope you'll remember this feeling the next time you want to steal something."

Your Turn

Has anything of yours ever been stolen? If so, how did that make you feel?

___

___

Prayer

God, I see a lot of stuff I'd like to have for my own. Show me how to work for what I want, and help me to remember what's mine and what's not. Amen.

STICKY FINGERS

Stealing isn't funny and it isn't right. God expects you to show respect for things that belong to other people. Follow the word wheel below to find a message Paul sent to the church of Ephesus (in Ephesians 4:28). Start with the circled letter on top of the wheel and read every other letter. Keep going around the circle until you return to the circled letter again.

(The solution is on page 248.)

HARD STUFF WITH OTHERS

God wants me to follow wise rules.

Remind the people to be subject to rulers and authorities, to be obedient, to be ready to do whatever is good.
– Titus 3:1

Pool Rules

Derek ignored the lifeguard's whistle as he ran beside the pool. After all, the lifeguard was his older brother, Keegan. With a cheery wave, Derek dove into the pool. When he came up, Keegan was waiting.

"What part of my whistle don't you understand?" Keegan asked him. "No running! No diving in this end!"

"You're not my boss, Mr. Big Man!"

"I am when you're in this pool," Keegan said.

Derek said, "You care more about your dumb rules than about your own brother."

"I do care about you, Peabrain. That's why I want you to follow the rules," Keegan said. "What if you slipped on the wet concrete or ran into somebody?"

"Big deal," Derek said.

"Last summer a kid dived into the shallow end and hit his head," Keegan said. "He'll be in a wheelchair for the rest of his life. Is that a big deal?"

"That's awful," Derek said in a small voice.

Keegan laid a hand on Derek's shoulder.

"I want you to have fun, but I want you to be safe, too," Keegan said. "No matter how old you are, there will always be rules for your own good."

"From now on I'll pay attention to the rules," Derek said.

"You'd better," Keegan said. "I'll be on break in fifteen minutes, and there's no rule against dunking your little brother."

Your Turn

If no one followed the rules, what would it be like in your school? In a ballgame? On the highway?

____

____

Prayer

Lord, help me follow the rules that make life safe and happy. Amen.

FOLLOW THE LEADERS

Jesus is the Ruler to obey above everyone else, but He gives us other leaders, too. These leaders help guide us in life. Jesus wants you to be obedient and respectful to them.

Fill in the blanks below to help you remember some of the leaders who watch over you each day. (If you need a hint, the picture to the right shows something this person might use in his or her job.)

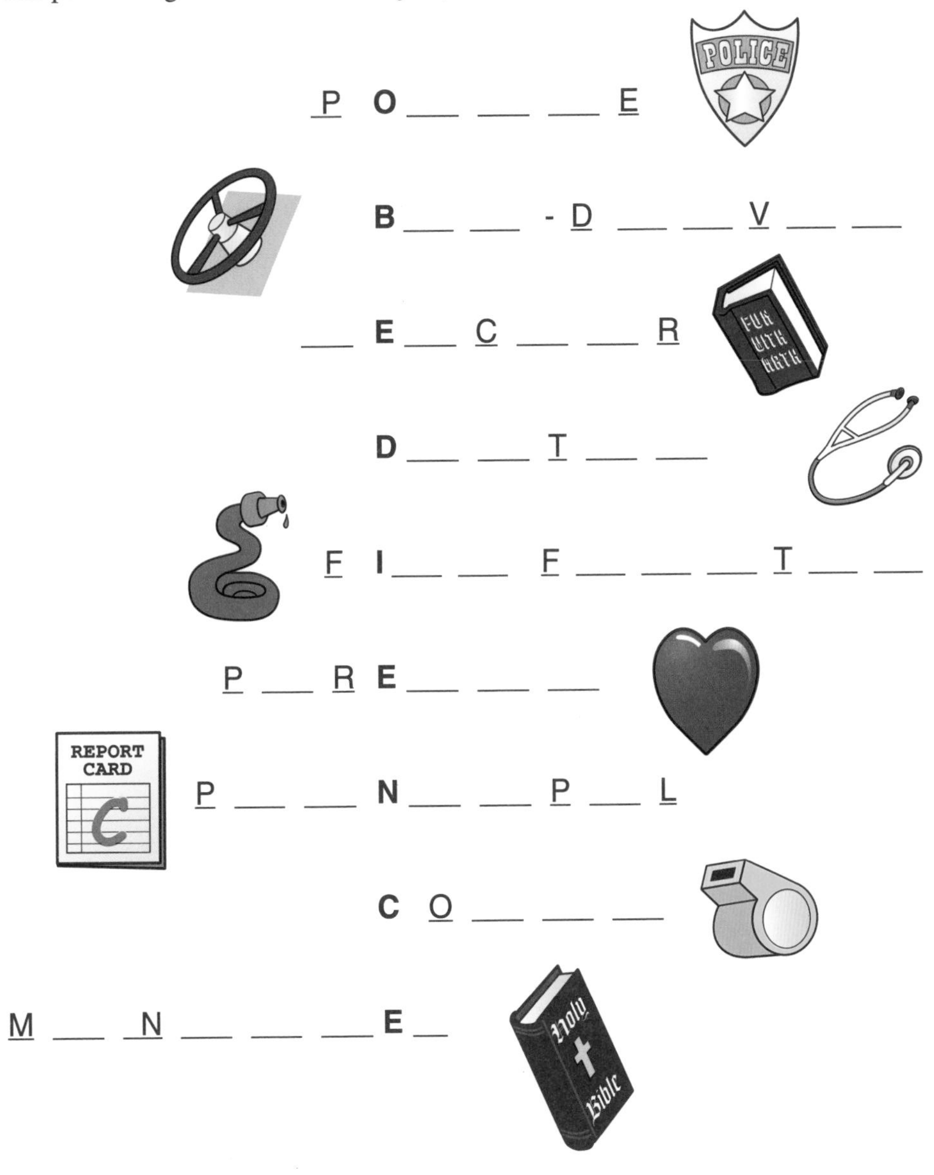

(The solution is on page 248.)

HARD STUFF WITH GOD

God wants me to admit my mistakes.

If we confess our sins, he is faithful and just and will forgive us our sins and purify us from all unrighteousness.

– 1 John 1:9

The Second Mistake

"I have some homework to do," Sam Kent said as he pulled back his chair from the dinner table.

"We need to talk to you first," said Mr. Kent.

Sam sat back down. His parents looked serious, and Sam wondered what was wrong.

Mrs. Kent laid a ticket stub on the table next to Sam's plate.

"I found that in your pocket while I was doing the laundry," his mother said. "It's a movie ticket stub from last Friday night, a ticket to *Blood Party*."

Sam stared at the stub. He couldn't think of anything to say.

"Remember I asked you on Saturday what movie you and your friends had gone to see?" Mr. Kent asked. "You lied to me, didn't you?"

"I'm sorry, Dad," Sam said. "We wanted to see a different movie, but it was sold out. I knew you wouldn't approve, but I went along with the crowd."

"What bothers us even more is that you lied about it," said Mrs. Kent. "Why didn't you tell us what happened?"

"I thought you'd be mad," Sam said.

Mr. Kent said, "Your mother and I know that sometimes people make bad choices. We'd have understood. It wouldn't have been a big deal."

"But you turned one mistake into two mistakes," said Mrs. Kent.

"I'm really sorry," Sam said. "I should have told you what happened."

"I believe you, son," said Mr. Kent. "Let's put this behind us now."

"I need to do one more thing," Sam said. "I need to tell God I'm sorry."

Your Turn

Why is it important to tell God about your mistakes when He already knows?

____

____

Prayer

God, mistakes don't go away just because I keep them secret. I'm always going to be honest with You. Amen.

COMING CLEAN

God loves you and doesn't want your sins to separate you from Him. If you sincerely tell God that you're sorry for your mistakes, He will eagerly forgive you. The Bible has many prayers that say "I'm sorry" to God. One of those prayers is Psalm 51. In these lines from Psalm 51, some of the words are wrong. You can fix this prayer by replacing each red word with the right word. (Here's some help. The right word and the wrong word rhyme with each other. So in the first line, replace "dove" with "love.")

PSALM 51 (selected verses from the New International Version)

Have Percy on me, O God, according to your unfailing dove;

according to your hate compassion knot out my transgressions.

Squash away all my iniquity and hens me from my fin.

For I glow my transgressions, and my grin is always adore me.

Surely you desire tooth in the inner darts; you leech me wisdom in the inmost place.

Create in me a sure tart, O God, and undo a steadfast spirit within me.

Restore to me the soy of your creation and grant me a drilling spirit, to sustain me.

Now that you've got the right words in place, read through the prayer

slowly and think about what it says.

(The solution is on page 248.)

HARD STUFF WITH GOD

God always watches over me.

Even though I walk through the valley of the shadow of death, I will fear no evil, for you are with me.

– Psalm 23:4

In God's Strong Hand

Nathan walked into the hospital room and looked around. Grandpa was lying in a bed with blinking machines hanging on the wall overhead.

"Hey, Nate," Grandpa called. "Come here and give an old man a hug."

Nathan stretched across the bed and hugged his grandfather.

"How are you doing?" Nathan asked.

"I feel fine," Grandpa said. "I'm having surgery tomorrow."

"I know," Nathan said. "Mom says it's kind of dangerous. Are you scared?"

"No," Grandpa said, smiling. "I'm not scared even a little bit."

"I'm scared," Nathan said in a small voice.

"Well, don't be," Grandpa said. "Jesus has been taking care of me my whole life, and Jesus won't let me down now."

"So, you'll be okay after the surgery?" Nathan asked.

Grandpa said, "I hope so. I'd like to have about 10 more summers to take you fishing. But everybody dies sooner or later. Even if I die tomorrow, I've had a good life with a lot of blessings."

Grandpa stuck out one hand palm up.

"God is holding me right there in the palm of His hand," Grandpa said. "Do you think God will accidentally drop me?"

"Never," Nathan said.

Grandpa nodded.

"That's right," Grandpa said. "So what should I be afraid of? God is the strongest one of all, and God's hand is holding me tight."

Your Turn

Of what are you most afraid? Have you talked to God about it?

____

____

Prayer

Jesus, when I'm afraid help me to remember that You're going to take care of me no matter what. Amen.

A MIGHTY FORTRESS IS OUR GOD!

The Bible uses all kinds of words to describe how God takes care of us and watches over us. These strong names for God can help you to remember that nothing in life or death is mightier than God!

See if you can fit these strong names into the crossword puzzle below.

REFUGE	GUARDIAN	SHEPHERD	SHELTER
SHIELD	PROTECTOR	ROCK	FORTRESS
DEFENDER	TOWER	HELPER	

(The solution is on page 248.)

HARD STUFF WITH GOD

Jesus has a place waiting for me in heaven.

Surely goodness and love will follow me all the days of my life, and I will dwell in the house of the Lord forever.

– Psalm 23:6

A House Made of Love

"Hi, Mom," Nathan said as his mother came into the house. "Where have you been?"

"I spent the afternoon at Grandpa's house," she said as she flopped wearily on the couch. "There are a lot of things to repair before we can sell the house."

Nathan's grandfather had died a few weeks before, just two days after surgery.

"I miss Grandpa," Nathan said.

"Me, too," his mother said.

Then Nathan asked, "Remember at Grandpa's funeral, the pastor said going to heaven is like moving into a beautiful new house? Do you think that's right?"

"Heaven is so wonderful that we can never find the words to describe it," Nathan's mother said. "But I guess it is a little like moving into a new house. Grandpa's old house has a leaky roof, and rain gets into the basement. The furnace is old, and the house gets cold in the winter."

"But now Grandpa's in a new house?" Nathan asked. "What's it like?"

His mother smiled.

"We won't know exactly what heaven's like until we get there," she said, "but we know it'll be better than our best dreams. Never too hot or too cold. Never lonely. No more sickness or pain or sadness. No more death."

Nathan decided that Grandpa must be happy in heaven. A house made of love would be just right for Grandpa.

Your Turn

What do you think heaven will be like?

____

____

Prayer

Lord, this world is a wonderful place, and You say that heaven is even better! Wow! What a great God You are! Amen.

THE BEST PLACE OF ALL

Nathan's mom is right. Nobody is completely sure what heaven will be like, but you can trust God and know it will be a wonderful place. Nobody knows you better than God, so God knows just what you need to be happy forever.

Even if you don't know everything about heaven, you can be pretty sure of some good things that will be there, and some bad things that definitely won't be there. Make an X through the things on this page that you believe will not be in heaven. Circle the things you believe will be there.

When you are finished, draw a picture that shows how you feel about heaven.

death love

sickness hate

life

happiness

fear

family joy peace

pain

Jesus music health

beauty laughter

MY OWN HARD STUFF

Big words won't make me any bigger.

But now you are proud, and you boast; all such boasting is wrong.
– James 4:16 TEV

The Best Batter in the Neighborhood

Luis picked up a bat and swung it a few times. He shook his head, dropped the bat and tried another.

"Come on! Come on!" yelled the pitcher. "You waiting for Christmas?"

As Luis walked slowly toward home plate, he thought, *I had to be a big shot. Why did I tell them I'm a great batter?*

Half an hour earlier, while the captains were choosing players, Luis had yelled, "Hey! If you want some runs, pick me! I can knock the hide off that ball! I'm the best batter in the whole neighborhood!"

Luis was always saying that kind of stuff. He wanted to have friends, and he thought bragging would make others like him.

This is going to be awful, Luis told himself as he planted his feet beside home plate. *I'm going to strike out and then everybody will be mad at me. Why do I have to brag all the time?*

Luis missed the first pitch and fouled the second. On the third pitch Luis slammed into the ball, and the ball sailed into right field. The fielder fumbled the catch and dropped the ball. Then he overthrew to second base and the ball rolled into tall grass outside the baseline. By the time the other team found the ball, Luis had run all the way home.

The team captain gave Luis a high-five and then he said, "You really are a great batter!"

Luis thought about it for a second and then said, "Nah, I'm really not a very good hitter. I just got lucky."

The captain shrugged and said, "Stick around after the game, and I'll give you some pointers."

"Yeah," said Luis. "I'll do that. I could use some help."

Your Turn

What is a better way to impress someone than bragging?

____

____

Prayer

Lord, I want people to like me for who I really am. Help me be myself without bragging or pretending. Amen.

THE REAL ME

Boasting is not the same thing as taking healthy pride in your accomplishments. Sometimes the difference is simply in your tone of voice or your attitude. Your words usually let others know when you're boasting and showing off. Some of these sentences are good ways to talk about your abilities and activities. Others are boasting. Can you tell the difference? Scratch out the boasting sentences. For the remaining sentences, write the blue letters on the blanks to make a message worth remembering.

Soccer is important to me, so I never goof off during practice.

I'm the fastest runner in the world. I leave everybody else in the dust.

I'm too short to get many rebounds, but I'm good at free throws.

I'm the only guy that dresses cool in this whole school.

My art teacher says my drawing is really improving.

Our softball team is in second place.

If you were as smart I am, you'd get straight A's too.

Check me out! Was that a great shot or what?

If you want, I can show you how to do some pretty good tricks on your skateboard.

___ ___ ___ ___ ___ ___ ___ ___ ___ ___ !

(The solution is on page 248.)

MY OWN HARD STUFF

It's better to be happy with what I have
than to envy what others have.

A heart at peace gives life to the body, but envy rots the bones.
– Proverbs 14:30

The Comic Book Collection

Rudy stared at his comic book collection and sighed. He had three boxes almost filled with comics. Each comic book was sealed carefully in a plastic bag to keep it in good condition. Rudy used to bring friends to his room to show off his collection. He'd pull out special issues and tell his friends how much each comic was worth.

Rudy used to be proud of his comic book collection. But not anymore. Not since he'd visited his cousin Garrett. While on vacation, Rudy's family had spent the night with relatives in another city. Rudy had never met Garrett before, but they were the same age and quickly became friends. When Garrett found out Rudy liked comic books, Garrett invited his cousin to see his own collection.

Rudy couldn't believe what an incredible collection Garrett had. Garrett had gotten a lot of his comics from his father, who was a collector when he was a boy. Some of Garrett's books were over 40 years old. Garrett even had a copy of Spider Man #1! Rudy's eyes almost popped out when he saw that.

As Rudy held Spider Man #1 in his hands, Garrett had said, "Tell me about your collection."

"Oh, it's not really a collection," Rudy mumbled. "It's just a few books I picked up here and there. You know, the usual stuff."

Rudy had been back from vacation for over a month, but he couldn't stop thinking of all the wonderful comics Garrett owned. Rudy's collection now seemed small and puny. At his favorite comic book shop, Rudy looked at the old issues, but he didn't have the money to buy them. Rudy wished he'd never met Garrett. He wished he'd never seen Garrett's collection. He didn't think he was ever going to enjoy comic books again.

Your Turn

Why is it so easy to envy what others have?

____

____

Prayer

God, help me be content with what I have and not spend all my time thinking about what I don't have. Amen.

THE ENVY MONSTER

Envy can make you feel awful. When you envy others, you want what you don't have and you lose interest in what you do have. Envy is a monster who loves to get hold of you and make you miserable.

Draw the Envy Monster below. Use your imagination to make it look horrible! Here are some ideas to get you started.

- The Envy Monster has lots of eyes for looking at things that belong to other people.
- The Envy Monster has long arms and grabby hands because he's always reaching for what doesn't belong to him.
- The Envy Monster has a big frown and an angry expression because he's never happy.

Is this a monster you want living in your heart?

MY OWN HARD STUFF

I can learn from others.

The way of a fool seems right to him,
but a wise man listens to advice.

– Proverbs 12:15

The Vacant Lot

Ike's dad lifted the lawn mower out of the trunk and set it on the sidewalk. He and Ike looked at the vacant lot. The grass was high, and the lot was scattered with fast-food cups and paper. Mr. Richards, who was on the neighborhood council, had called and asked if Ike would like to mow this lot during the summer.

Ike's dad said, "Let me make a suggestion. Before you start the mower, walk over the lot and pick up the garbage. It will only take a few minutes, and you'll save time in the end."

But Ike had his own ideas. As soon as his dad drove away, Ike started the mower. Picking up garbage was too slow. He wanted to get the job done quickly. He pushed the mower through the tall grass. Whenever he came to a paper cup, he ran over it. As he reached the end of the lot, he turned the mower and started back.

When he turned the mower, Ike saw that the papers had been cut into tiny bits and scattered across the ground. Maybe his dad was right about picking up the garbage first! Now he'd have to pick up hundreds of scraps of paper.

Just then, a loud clunk came from under the mower and it stopped running. Ike saw that he had hit a brick half-buried in the tall grass. He picked up the brick and threw it angrily onto the sidewalk. Then he pulled the cord on the mower, but it wouldn't start. He pulled and pulled until he was sweaty and out of breath.

Ike looked at the messy lot and the broken mower. He wished he had taken his father's advice.

Your Turn

Why is it easy to be stubborn about doing things your own way?

____

____

Prayer

God, I don't have to do things the way other people tell me to, but I'm going to listen anyway. Maybe I can learn something good. Amen.

WISE WORDS FOR WISE PEOPLE

Did you know there's a book in the Bible that is crammed with good advice? The Book of Proverbs is filled with short pieces of advice that will keep you out of trouble and make your life much better. Some of these proverbs (a "proverb" is a wise saying) are funny, some are sad, and others may leave you scratching your head. Here are a few nuggets from Proverbs to give you the general idea:

Laziness: Lazy hands make a man poor, but diligent hands bring wealth. (Proverbs 10:4)

Kind Words: Pleasant words are a honeycomb, sweet to the soul and healing to the bones. (Proverbs 16:24)

Stopping an Argument: A gentle answer turns away wrath, but a harsh word stirs up anger. (Proverbs 15:1)

Anger: For as churning the milk produces butter, and as twisting the nose produces blood, so stirring up anger produces strife. (Proverbs 30:33)

Honesty: An honest answer is like a kiss on the lips. (Proverbs 24:26)

Neighbors: He who despises his neighbor sins, but blessed is he who is kind to the needy. (Proverbs 14:21)

Making Money: Dishonest money dwindles away, but he who gathers money little by little makes it grow. (Proverbs 13:11)

And here's one more proverb with advice, but you'll have to decipher this one. 1 stands for A, 2 stands for B, 11 stands for K, and so on. You can figure it out. Go for it! The solution is on page 249.

1-16-16-12-25 25-15-21-18 8-5-1-18-20 20-15

____

9-14-19-20-18-21-3-20-9-15-14 1-14-4 25-15-21-18

____

5-1-18-19 20-15 23-15-18-4-19 15-6

____

11-14-15-23-12-5-4-7S-5.

____

– Proverbs 23:12

God doesn't like lying.

Do not lie to each other.

– Colossians 3:9

The Excuse

"I wish I hadn't watched TV last night," Ellis said as he and his friend Norman entered their school. "I didn't get my science report done and it's due today."

The boys stopped at their lockers and hung up their coats.

"I'll just have to come up with a good excuse," Ellis said. "Maybe I'll tell Mrs. Corrigan that our dog got hit by a car and we had to take him to the vet last night. She'll probably give me more time, don't you think?"

"Maybe," Norman said. "She's a nice teacher."

"Yeah," Ellis agreed. "She's so nice she might call my parents to ask how the dog's doing."

Ellis hung his coat in the locker.

"I know!" he said. "I'll pretend that my computer crashed. Do you think that will fool her?"

Norman turned to face his friend.

"Ellis," he asked, "why don't you just tell Mrs. Corrigan the truth?"

"I'll get in trouble," Ellis protested.

"You might get in more trouble for lying," Norman said. "Besides, won't you feel crummy telling a lie? That's a lousy way to treat Mrs. Corrigan."

When Ellis got to science class, he told Mrs. Corrigan that he didn't have his report. He asked if he could turn it in tomorrow.

"Do you have a good reason?" Mrs. Corrigan asked.

"No," Ellis said. "I just put it off too long."

Mrs. Corrigan nodded and smiled at Ellis.

"Bring it in tomorrow," she said. "I'll take off five points for lateness, but if you do a good job you can still get an A."

Your Turn

Does lying solve problems or cause problems? Why?

____

____

Prayer

God, everything You do and say is the truth. Help me to be more like You. Amen.

THE EASY WAY

One lie usually leads to another. You have to keep lying to cover up the lies you told before. Lies get you all tangled up! But the truth untangles your life. When you tell the truth, everything is so much simpler, and when you know the truth of God's love, everything is so much happier.

Here's what Jesus has to say about the truth. To figure out the message, read the grid coordinates. Fill in the letters on the blanks. The first number in a coordinate is always the bottom number. For instance, 2,4 is L.

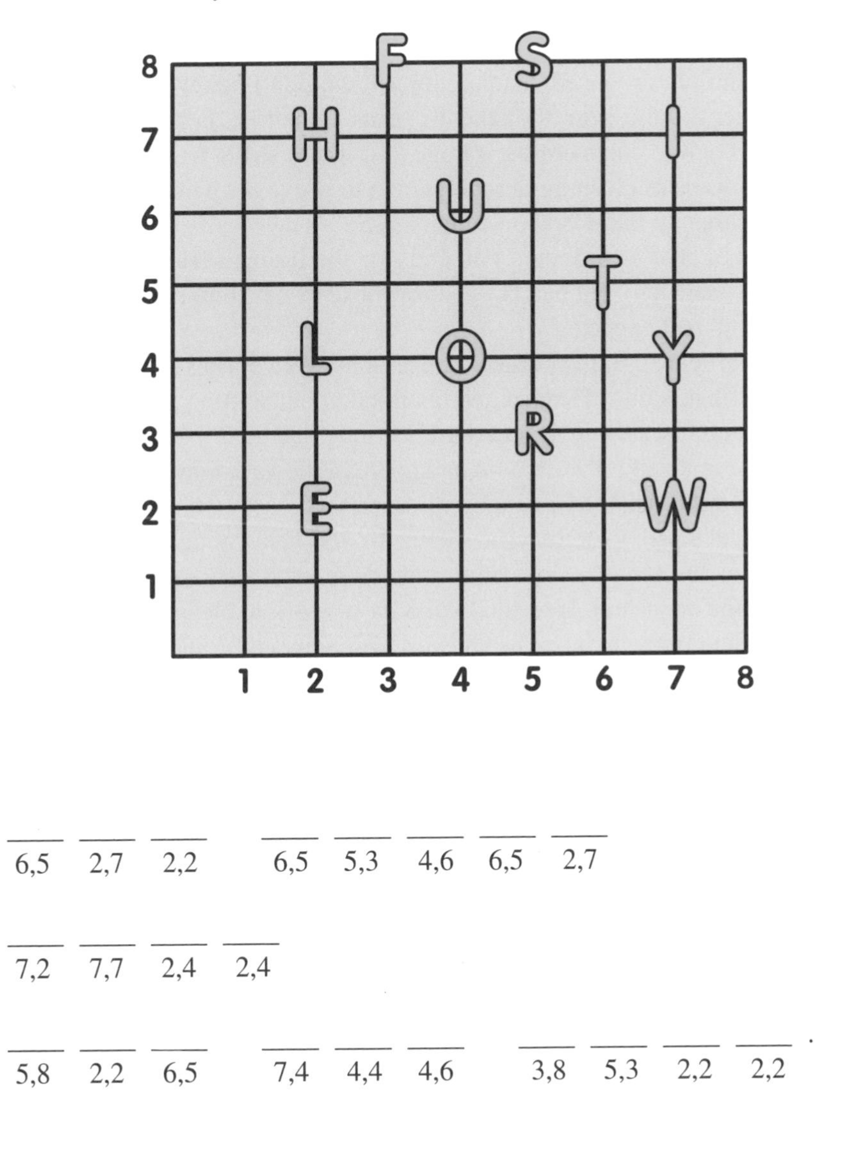

(The solution is on page 249.)

MY OWN HARD STUFF

Just talking about something won't get it done.

All hard work brings a profit, but mere talk leads only to poverty.
– Proverbs 14:23

More Than Talk

My parents are the meanest people in the world, Enrique told himself as he moved boxes in the garage. All he wanted was a dog. But Enrique's parents said he wouldn't take care of a dog.

Even after Enrique promised, his parents still wouldn't believe him. They said Enrique never did the work to make his plans come true. For instance, he'd promised months ago to clean out the garage, but it was still a mess.

So now Enrique was cleaning out the garage to prove his parents wrong. He'd show them that he knew how to finish a job.

Enrique peeked into a cardboard box and saw the in-line skates he got for his birthday two years ago. He had begged for those skates, but in-line skating was harder than he had expected.

A dusty guitar leaned in the corner. The lessons were boring and practicing made Enrique's fingers hurt. He changed his mind about starting a rock band.

Next to the guitar was a dirty aquarium. Enrique had gotten tired of the goldfish when he realized how often he had to clean the aquarium. After a few weeks, he dumped the fish into a pond at the cemetery.

Maybe Enrique's parents were right. Maybe he was better at talking than working. But he really wanted a dog. How could he prove he was ready to change?

He studied the aquarium. It would take a lot of work to clean off the dried scum and get it set up again, but if he showed his parents he could take care of fish, they might let him have a dog. Enrique decided to get started on the aquarium right away. He picked it up, then stopped and looked at the junk piled all over the garage.

"Maybe I'd better finish cleaning the garage first," Enrique said. "Then I'll fix up the aquarium."

Your Turn

Have you ever made plans that turned into a lot of work? What did you do?

____

____

Prayer

God, talking is easy, but working gets things done. Show me how to make my plans come true. Amen.

GETTING THE JOB DONE

The Bible tells the story of a man named Nehemiah who had a big job to do. The city of Jerusalem needed tall, strong walls all around the city to protect the people from their enemies. Building the walls was a difficult job that called for weeks of hard work. Many people didn't want to help, and enemies threatened to attack if Nehemiah and his friends started building. Still, Nehemiah wouldn't give up. He gathered the materials needed for the work and got the people organized. It wasn't easy, but Nehemiah kept working until the walls were finished.

In these scrambled words are some of the things Nehemiah needed to get his job done. Unscramble them and fill in each block below with one word. Then circle the things that might help you get your jobs done. The solution is on page 249.

WATES	TEONS
KROW	NLAP
MTRROA	ELPH
HIFAT	MRAHEM
ETMI	TPENCIAE

GETTING TO
KNOW JESUS

Jesus expects me to obey Him.

Why do you call me, "Lord, Lord" and do not do what I say?
– Luke 6:46

Learning to Obey

"Heel," Judd said as his dog, Rex, ran around in a tight circle and then chased a butterfly across the yard.

"Rex, if you want a treat, you'd better get back here," Judd called.

When he heard the word "treat," Rex ran back to Judd and stood panting.

"Heel!" Judd commanded.

Rex rose up on his hind legs and planted his front paws on Judd's chest. Rex licked Judd's face.

"I love you," Judd said, laughing,"but you are dumber than a bag of rocks."

Rex wagged his tail and bounded across the yard to sniff at a molehill. Judd sat on the grass and watched Rex exploring the yard.

The dog trotted over to Judd and flopped down beside him. Rex laid his head in his master's lap, and Judd rubbed behind his floppy ears.

"I'm not just trying to boss you around," Judd said. "I'm trying to take care of you. If you'll obey me, you and I can take long walks around the neighborhood. We can go to the lake and chase rabbits. But not until you learn to do what I say."

Rex looked sadly at Judd.

"I'm not mad at you, Rex," Judd said. "I guess Jesus has the same problem trying to get me to obey. He's my Lord and I'm supposed to do what He tells me."

Rex raised one ear as if he understood every word.

"When I obey my Lord, Jesus and I get along fine," Judd said. "But when I disobey, it always gets me in trouble. Jesus wants me to obey so He can take care of me."

Judd stood up and said, "Let's try it again, Rex. Sooner or later you're going to get this right. Heel!"

Your Turn

Jesus is your Lord. Does that mean He likes to boss you around? Why or why not?

____

____

Prayer

Jesus, Your teaching is just what I need to live a safe and happy life. Help me learn to obey Your words. Amen.

WHAT WOULD YOU DO?

In John 9 there is a story about Jesus meeting a blind man. Use your imagination to put yourself in the story. In your mind, picture each part of the story. Think about the questions and what you would have done if you were the blind man.

One day, Jesus and the disciples came upon a man who had been blind since birth. In his whole life he had never seen a bird or a star. Jesus wanted to help this man, so He spat on the ground, made some mud and rubbed it on the man's eyes.

If you were the blind man, would you have let Jesus rub spit and mud on your eyes? Would you have wondered why He chose that way to heal you? After all, Jesus had healed some other blind people just by talking to them–why rub spit and dirt on you? Can you trust Jesus even when you don't understand what He's doing?

Then Jesus told the man to go to the Pool of Siloam and wash the mud from his eyes.

Would you have wondered why Jesus didn't heal you instantly as He did for other blind people? Why would Jesus make you walk across town to a pool to get your sight back? Would you have believed it would really work? Would you have gone?

So the man got up and started to the Pool of Siloam. He must have looked foolish with mud caked on his eyes. Maybe he could hear people in the crowd laughing at him and making jokes as he walked along.

If you had been the blind man, would you have changed your mind? Would you have been so embarrassed that you rubbed the mud off your face and went back to begging? Do you think you would have walked all the way to the pool?

When the man got to the pool, he splashed water on his face and washed away the mud. When he opened his eyes, he could see. For the first time in his whole life, the man could see the world around him.

What if the man hadn't trusted Jesus? What if he had refused to let Jesus rub mud on his eyes? What if he had said, "No, I won't go all the way to the Pool of Siloam. I feel silly with mud on my face"? How would the story have turned out? How do you think things will turn out for you if you obey Jesus? What if you decide not to trust Jesus? Would Jesus ever ask you to do things that wouldn't turn out for your good?

JESUS, THE SAVIOR

Jesus saves us to live forever with God.

And we have seen and testify that the Father has sent his Son to be the Savior of the world.

– 1 John 4:14

The One and Only

"Remember that story on TV about those firefighters who helped people get out of the burning building in New York?" Harley asked.

"Yeah," Drew said. "Those firefighters were real heroes."

"Here's what I'm wondering," Harley said. "Were the firefighters saviors to those people?"

"I guess so," Drew said. "They did save them."

"Right," said Harley. "Firefighters save people all the time. So do cops and doctors and lifeguards. How is Jesus different from those other saviors?"

"That's easy," Drew told his friend. "We talked about this in Sunday school. Jesus is the only one who saves people forever."

"What does that mean?"

"Let's pretend there's a guy named Joe," Drew said, "and a doctor saves Joe from a heart attack. Then what happens to Joe?"

"I guess he goes on living."

"How long?" Drew asked.

"Uh, 50 more years."

"Then what?"

"Then Joe dies."

"Right," said Drew. "So the doctor saved Joe for another 50 years, but he couldn't save Joe forever. Only one person can save Joe forever."

"I get it!" Harley said. "People can save each other for a while, but Jesus is the one who can save us to live in heaven forever."

"Exactly," Drew agreed. "There are lots of heroes in the world, but there's only one Jesus. Other people might be rescuers, but Jesus is the only true Savior."

Your Turn

Do you trust Jesus to save you forever? Why or why not?

____

____

Prayer

Jesus, I'm glad You put heroes and helpers in the world, but You're my biggest hero. Amen.

NO OTHER SAVIOR

Do you sometimes forget that Jesus is the only one who can truly save you? Here's a way to make a reminder for you and your friends.
You'll need a piece of paper and a pair of scissors for this paper trick.

1. Fold down the top left corner of your paper.

2. Then fold down the top right corner.

3. Fold the left side over the right side.

4. Cut the paper as shown and throw away the part on the right.

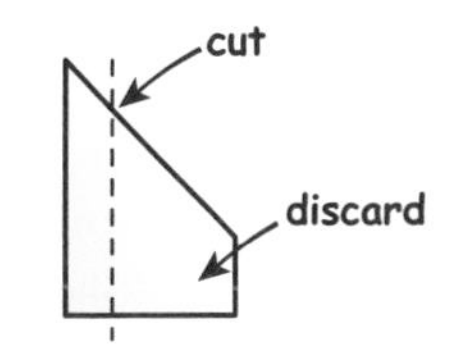

5. Open up the folded part and you will find a reminder of the Savior!

JESUS, THE GOOD SHEPHERD

Jesus always watches over me.

"I am the good shepherd."

– John 10:11

The Lost Lamb

"Did you hear that?" Uncle Clark asked. He turned off the engine of the pickup truck and said to Bruce, "Listen hard."

Bruce listened through the open window of the truck. Bruce loved visiting his uncle's sheep ranch in the summer. In the distance he saw hundreds of sheep grazing on the hills. Somewhere a dog was barking, but that's all Bruce heard.

"Over there in those rocks," Uncle Clark said, getting out of the truck. "I heard a sheep cry."

Some of the stones were as large as the truck. They were jumbled together and thorny bushes grew between them. Uncle Clark walked around the rocks quietly. A soft "baaa" came from somewhere in the thorns.

"Now I hear it," Bruce said.

"Sounds like a lamb," Uncle Clark said.

Uncle Clark got down on his hands and knees, squeezing between the stones. In a few minutes he pulled a black and white lamb from the thorns. He held the lamb firmly, checking it over from head to tail.

"No harm done," Uncle Clark said. "This little guy will be fine."

"But what about you?" Bruce asked. He saw bloody scratches on his uncle's arms where the thorns had stabbed him.

"It goes with the job," Uncle Clark said. "I'm a shepherd, and I take care of my sheep. They come first. Now let's get this lamb back to the flock."

Uncle Clark got behind the wheel and Bruce rode with the lamb on his lap. The lamb seemed peaceful and happy. Bruce scratched the wool between its ears.

"You're a lucky lamb," Bruce whispered, "to have such a good shepherd watching out for you."

Your Turn

Jesus says He will be your Good Shepherd. What does that mean to you?

___

___

Prayer

Jesus, thanks for keeping a close eye on me. I know You've got a lot of people to watch over, and I'm so glad You never forget about me. Amen.

WHO IS YOUR SHEPHERD?

There are 150 psalms, but Psalm 23 is many people's favorite. Some call it the "shepherd psalm" because it compares God to a loving shepherd.

The purple words in the psalm need to replaced with the right words. The right word will rhyme with the wrong word. For instance, you will replace "mean" with "green." When you've got all the right words in place, read slowly through Psalm 23 to see if it reminds you of Jesus.

Psalm 23

The Lord is my leopard, I shall not be in haunt.

He makes me lie down in mean pastures,
he leads me beside riot waters, he restores
my goal.

He slides me in wraths of righteousness for
his fame's sake.

Even though I talk through the galley of the
shadow of death,

I will gear no evil, for you are with me;
your nod and your laugh, they comfort me.

You prepare a cable before me in the presence of my enemies.

You anoint my head with soil; my cup overflows.

Surely goodness and love will swallow me all the days of my life,
and I will swell in the mouse of the Lord forever.

(The solution is on page 249.)

JESUS, THE BREAD OF LIFE

Jesus fills me with the good life that comes from God.

"I am the bread of life."

– John 6:35

A Loaf of Love

John looked up from his homework and sniffed the air. He followed the warm, sweet scent into the kitchen.

"It smells good when you make bread," he told his mother.

Mrs. Grey said, "When I was growing up, my mother taught me to make bread, and her mother taught her. Someday, I'll teach you."

"How long have people been making bread?" John asked.

"A long, long time," Mrs. Grey said. "I'm sure Jesus grew up eating His mother's homemade bread."

"I like bologna on my bread," John said. "What kind of sandwiches did Jesus eat?"

Mrs. Grey laughed. "No sandwiches back then. Bread was the meal," she said.

John tried to imagine eating bread without bologna or peanut butter.

"Oh, people would eat a little cheese or a piece of fish on the side, maybe a few figs and olives," Mrs. Grey added, "but bread was the most important food. It was bread that kept people from starving."

Mrs. Grey took a long, golden loaf of bread from the oven and shook it gently from the pan.

"That's why Jesus said, 'I am the bread of life.' Jesus is the most important thing in life. Nothing else matters more than Him and nothing but Jesus can give us true life."

Mrs. Grey cut two fat slices from the steaming loaf and laid them on a plate.

"Do you want honey or jam?" she asked.

"No, thanks," said John. "Your bread is good enough all by itself."

Your Turn

Food gives you health and life. What does Jesus give you?

____

____

Prayer

Thank You for giving me food so I can live today, God. Thank You even more for giving me Jesus so I can live forever. Amen.

FIRST THINGS FIRST

There are many things you need in life. Look at the list below and decide what things are most important to you. Put a #1 beside the thing you need most in life, then a #2 beside the second most important thing. Work through the whole list. When you finish, ask someone else to give his or her own answers on the same list. Compare your answers. Did you agree on everything? Did you agree on what comes first?

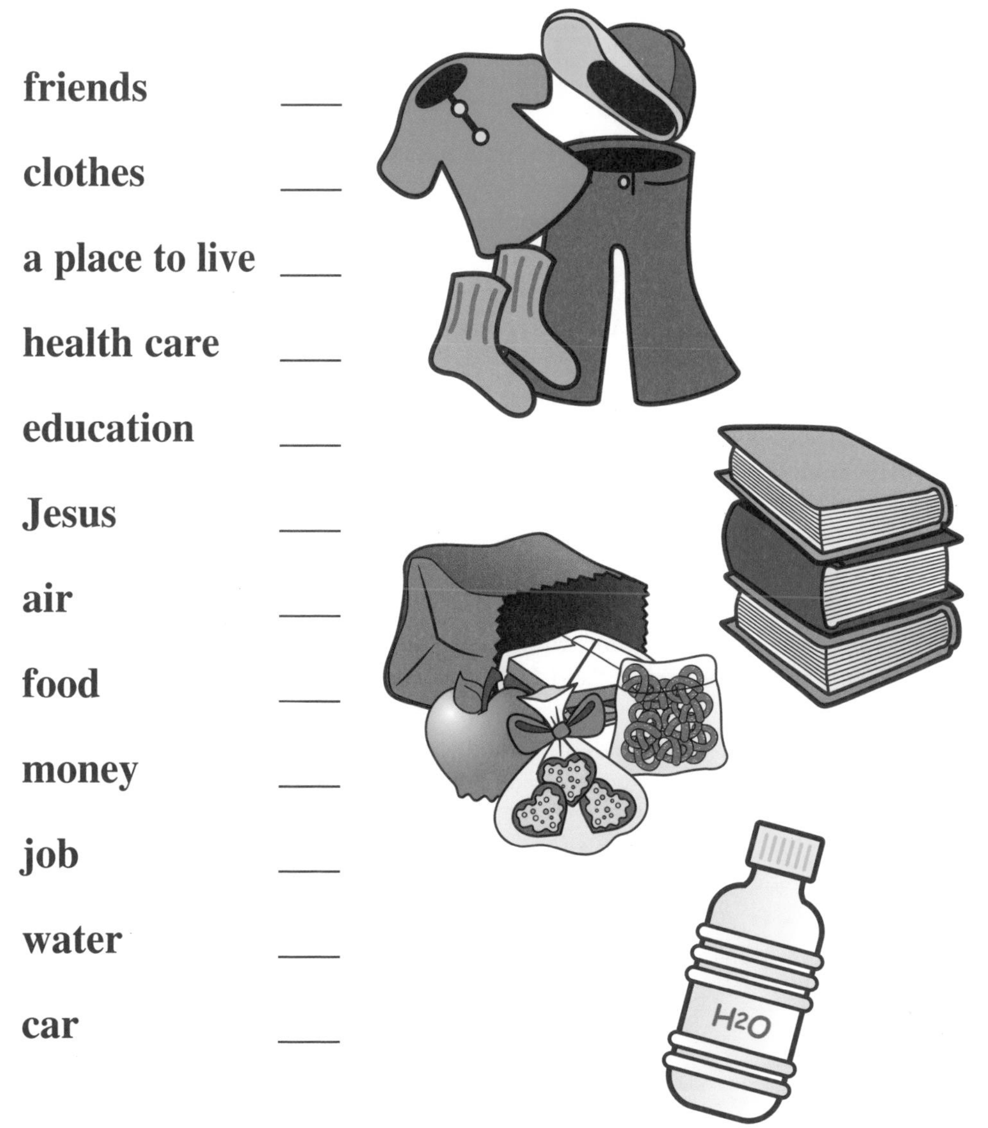

friends ___

clothes ___

a place to live ___

health care ___

education ___

Jesus ___

air ___

food ___

money ___

job ___

water ___

car ___

JESUS, THE DOOR

Jesus brings us to God.

"I am the door; if anyone enters through Me, he shall be saved."
– John 10:9 NASB

An Open and Shut Case

Jorge Ayala and his father lifted the front door from the hinges and laid it carefully on the picnic table. Jorge's father brushed on white paint in long strokes.

"When we finish," he said, "we'll let it dry for a couple of hours. We'll hang the door before we go to bed."

Jorge said, "That's good. I feel safer at night when the door is closed and locked."

"Sure," his father agreed. "A door has two jobs. One job is to protect us by keeping robbers outside."

"What's the other job?" Jorge asked.

"To let people in," Mr. Ayala said with a smile. "You don't expect your friends to come down the chimney, do you?"

Jorge laughed. "Here, let me take a turn," he said.

As Jorge spread the white paint evenly over the wood, he remembered something he'd read in his Bible.

"Jesus called Himself a door," Jorge said. "I didn't understand that before, but I get it now. Jesus is like a closed door keeping evil things from getting into my life."

Mr. Ayala nodded.

"And Jesus is an open door letting God's love come into my life."

"Yep," agreed Mr. Ayala, "and Jesus is the open door that lets us into heaven."

Jorge's father studied the door. "Good job," he said. "You're a fine painter, but I'll bet you don't know what painters do while they wait for the paint to dry."

Jorge shook his head.

"We sit under a tree," Mr. Ayala said, "and we drink lemonade."

Your Turn

Can you name some good things that have come into your life because of Jesus?

____

____

Prayer

Jesus, I know You will be a strong door to protect me today from hurts and sins. Please be an open door, too, so that all of God's blessings can come to me. Amen.

THE DOOR TO GOD

Jesus is the one who leads you to God and opens the way into heaven. You can know this is true because Jesus said so! Find out what Jesus said about Himself by reading His message on the word wheel. Start with the circled letter at the top of the wheel and move to the right. Skip the second letter, read the next one and so on, reading every other letter all the way around the wheel. When you've gone around the wheel twice and you end up at the period, you'll have the whole message.

(The solution is on page 249.)

JESUS, THE LIGHT OF THE WORLD

Jesus opens my eyes to real life.

"I am the light of the world."

– John 8:12

The Darkest Dark

"When I turn out the lights, it may be a little frightening," said the park ranger.

Kyle's family was touring a cave in a national park. Hidden electrical lights made the cave beautiful and kept the tourists safe on the path. Now the ranger was going to let them see what the cave was like without lights.

"This will be the darkest dark of your whole life," the guide told them.

"Oooooohhh, darker than midnight," Kyle whispered to his little brother, Bryan. "Try not to cry, Bryan, in the spooky, creepy dark."

But when the ranger flipped the switch, Kyle caught his breath. This darkness was so deep it swallowed up everything. Kyle knew his family was only inches away, but he felt completely alone in the world.

When the ranger spoke again, Kyle couldn't tell which direction his voice was coming from.

"Without the light we'd never find our way out," asked the guide. "We'd be lost in here until someone came to save us."

After the lights came back and the group was following the ranger along the winding path, Bryan said to Kyle, "That really was a little scary."

"Yeah," Kyle agreed. "It made me think of something my Sunday school teacher told me. Mr. Allen said the whole world was lost in the dark until Jesus came to light our way back to God."

"I guess not having Jesus would be the real darkest dark," Bryan said.

Your Turn

How does Jesus help you see the world in a new way?

____

____

Prayer

The dark is okay for sleeping, but today I want to run and play and see all the beautiful things around me. Thanks for being the light of my life, Jesus! Amen.

WALKING IN THE LIGHT

Have you ever stubbed your toe in the dark? Ouch! Jesus doesn't want you to stumble and trip in the way you live, so He gives you light for living every day. There's a promise from Jesus in the mixed-up letters below. It will take some work to figure out the promise, but it's worth it!

First, scratch out every P.

Now scratch out every Q and Y.

Change every X to L.

Change every C to O.

Change every J to E.

WPHYCPJVQJR FCQXPXYCQWS QMYPJ

____

WIYPXQX NJPVQJR WAXYQPK IQPN DQYAPRKNJSS,

____

BQUYPT WIQXPX HPQAVJ TPYQHJ XIQGPHT

____

CQPF XPIQFJ.

____

(The solution is on page 249.)

JESUS, THE VINE

God wants me to stay connected to Jesus.

"I am the vine; you are the branches."

– John 15:5

Keeping Connected

Kevin Walker stood at the back door holding a long, broken branch. His mother frowned at the leafy branch that held several clusters of tiny, green grapes.

"What happened?" she asked.

"Ruff and I were chasing the ball around and we accidentally crashed into your grape vines," Kevin said apologetically. "I guess this branch got broken off."

Kevin and Ruff the dog both looked at Mrs. Parker with sad eyes.

"You didn't hurt yourself, did you?" Mrs. Parker asked.

"No, I'm fine," Kevin said. "Can we do anything with this branch? Is there any way to keep it alive so the grapes can ripen?"

Mrs. Parker looked at her son thoughtfully.

She asked Kevin, "Do you remember what Jesus said about grapevines?"

Kevin thought for a moment.

"I think so," Kevin answered. "Didn't He say that He is like a vine and we Christians are like His branches?"

"That's right," Mrs. Walker said.

"As long as we stick to Christ, He'll fill us with His life. But if we break away from Him, we shrivel up and die inside."

Kevin looked at the broken-off branch in his hand. Already, the leaves were starting to droop limply.

"So what do I do with this branch?" Kevin asked.

"Throw it on the fire pile," his mother said. "That branch has no life of its own. We'll get our grapes from the branches that hang on to the vine."

She started back into the house. Over her shoulder she added, "At least we will if you and Ruff find some other place to play ball."

Your Turn

Jesus says that you will bear fruit if you stick to Him. What do you think He means by "fruit"?

____

____

Prayer

Jesus, You're the vine and I want to be one of Your branches. You hang on to me, and I'll hang on to You–forever! Amen.

BRANCHING OUT

As long as you are connected to Jesus, your life will be full and happy. How can you be sure to hang on to your Vine? Here are some ways to keep connected to Jesus, but you'll have to unscramble them. After you get the words straightened out, write them on the leaves of the vine. The solution is on page 249.

Following Jesus keeps me on the right path.

"I am the way."

– John 14:6

The Long Shortcut

Barry and Lyle could hardly wait to get to the cool, country stream and the swimming hole their uncle had told them about. They were wearing old shorts so they could leap right into the rocky pool.

"It's a bit of a walk," Uncle Ollie had told them, "but if you stay on the path you'll find it."

Barry mopped sweat from his face and said, "I'll bet there's a shorter way to get to the creek. It looks like the trail curves left up ahead. We can probably cut through the woods here and save a bunch of walking."

"I don't know," Lyle said. "Uncle Ollie said to follow the path."

"Come on," Barry urged, pushing through the bushes that grew beside the path. "How hard can it be to find a stream? All we have to do is head downhill. We'll listen for the running water."

Lyle thought about how good the cool, fresh water would feel and he followed Barry into the brush.

Two hours later Barry and Lyle still hadn't reached the swimming hole. Barry flopped down in some green vines and looked at the brier scratches on his bare legs.

"I guess we're lost," Barry admitted.

"And it's getting late," Lyle added. "We're just going to have to go back the way we came and hope we can get back to the farm before dark."

"Back through those blackberry briers?" Barry moaned. "If only we'd stayed on the path. I'm hot and tired. I'm scratched up. We never found the creek. How could this get any worse?"

"You'll find out in a few hours," Lyle told him. "You're sitting in poison ivy."

Your Turn

Can you think of a time when you didn't follow Jesus and it led you into trouble?

____

____

Prayer

Jesus, You know the way I should go in life. Help me follow wherever You lead. Amen.

FINDING YOUR WAY

Life has many twists and turns, but as long as you follow Jesus, you'll always be on the right path. Need some practice following Jesus? Try the maze below! You'll always make the right turn as long as you follow J-E-S-U-S.

(The solution is on page 249.)

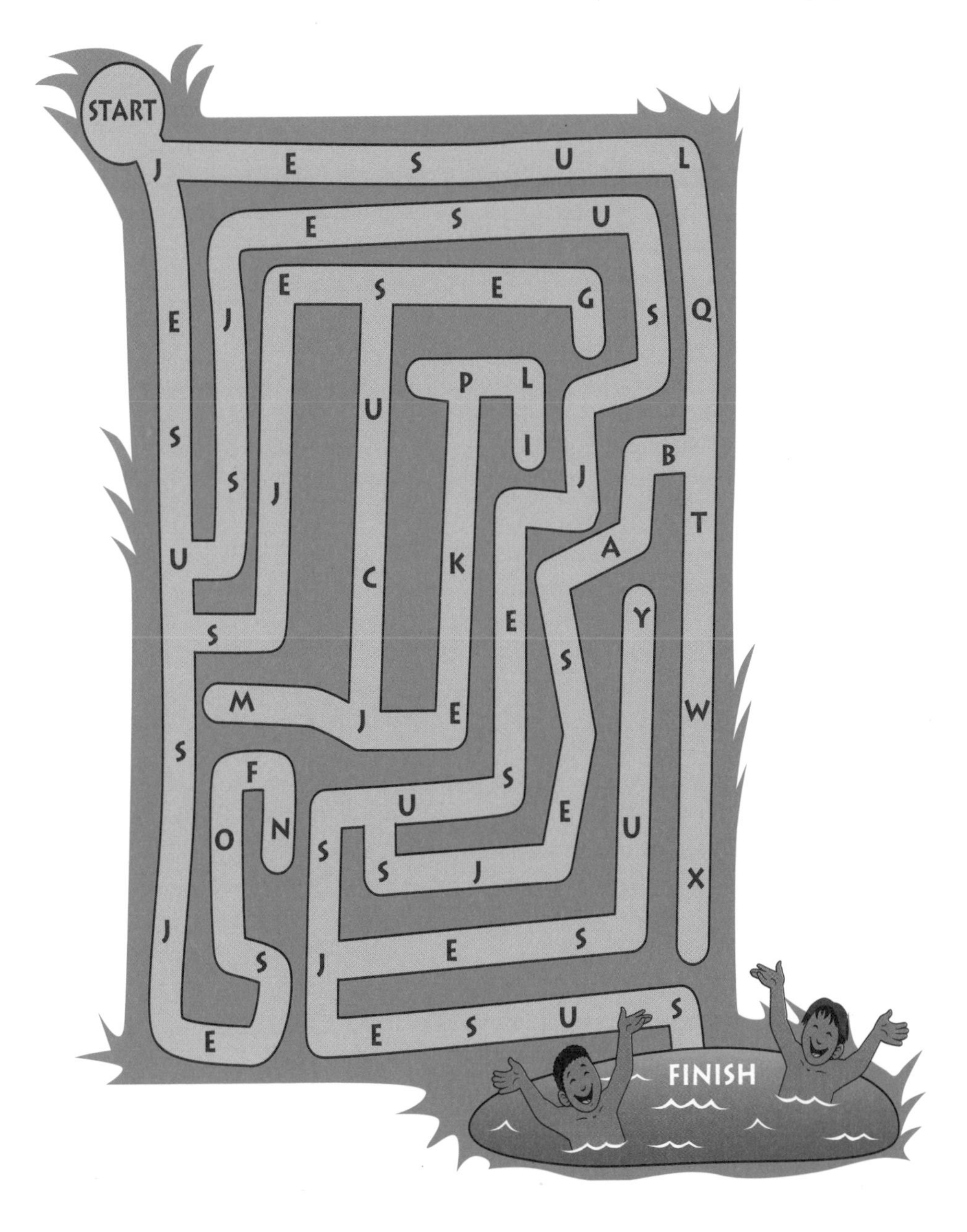

JESUS, THE FRIEND OF THE HUNGRY

Jesus doesn't want anyone to go without food.

"I have compassion for these people; they have already been with me three days and have nothing to eat."

– Mark 8:2

Extra Groceries

Jamal looked up and down the aisles of the supermarket until he found his mother pushing her cart. He went to her and dropped a can of tuna into the cart.

"Is it okay if we buy some tuna?" he asked.

"You don't like tuna," his mother said.

"No, I don't," Jamal admitted. "I'd still like to buy it. I'll pay you for it when we get home."

"You don't have to pay for groceries," Jamal's mother said. "Just tell me why you want to take home a can of tuna."

"I don't want to take it home," Jamal said. "I want to leave it here. We'll put it in the big box by the front door, the box where they collect food for the poor."

"Oh, I see," his mother said. "You want to help hungry people."

Jamal shrugged.

"I used to think that all hungry people lived in other countries far away," Jamal said, "but I found out there are people here who don't have enough to eat. The food they collect here in the supermarket helps people who live nearby. Jesus fed hungry people, didn't He?"

"Yes, He did," Jamal's mother said. "Here's what we'll do. You can pay me for this can of tuna when we get home, and you can go get three more cans off the shelf. I'll pay for those, and we'll leave all four in the box for the hungry."

"That's great!" Jamal said.

Jamal was sure some family would be glad to get that tuna, and Jesus would be glad, too.

Your Turn

Can you think of any ways to feed hungry people?

____

____

Prayer

Jesus, thanks for making sure there's enough food on my table every day. Show me how to share with people who don't have enough to eat. Amen.

WORKING WITH GOD

When you help feed hungry people, you are acting like Jesus and you are sharing in God's work. This message from Psalm 146:7 can remind you of what God is doing in the world.

Use the number code to read this message.

1 = T	2 = H	3 = R	4 = O	5 = E
6 = L	7 = S	8 = F	9 = D	10 = V
11 = G	12 = I	13 = U	14 = N	15 = Y

1-2-5 6-4-3-9 11-12-10-5-7

___

8-4-4-9 1-4

___

1-2-5 2-13-14-11-3-15

___

(The solution is on page 249.)

JESUS, THE FRIEND OF THE SICK

Jesus watches over the sick.

The whole town gathered at the door, and Jesus healed many who had various diseases.

– Mark 1:33-34

Touching Lepers

"What's a leper?" Chris asked, looking up from his Bible. "Isn't that an animal?"

"You're thinking of a leopard," his brother Adam told him. "A leper is someone who has leprosy. Leprosy is a skin disease."

"Like zits?" Chris asked.

"No, leprosy is a zillion times worse," Adam explained. "Lepers get terrible sores. Sometimes their fingers and toes fall off. Their skin sort of rots."

"Gross," Chris said. "I just read a story about Jesus making a leper get well."

"Back in the Bible days, it was awful for lepers," Adam said. "People were afraid of catching the disease, so they didn't want lepers around. A person with leprosy couldn't stay with his family. He had to go off and live alone."

"They must have been lonely and sad," Chris said.

"Yeah," Adam agreed. "If lepers came into town, people might throw rocks at them just to drive them off. Nobody was supposed to touch a leper."

"But Jesus did," Chris said. "Jesus touched the leper and made him well."

"That's because Jesus loves everybody," Adam said. "Jesus loves the people nobody else wants to have around. Jesus was always kind to the sick. Jesus helped the blind, the crippled, the deaf, people who couldn't talk. One time He cured a woman who was all bent over and couldn't stand up straight."

"And lepers, too," Chris said. "Don't forget the lepers."

"There's nobody Jesus doesn't love," Adam said, "and there's nobody Jesus is afraid to touch."

Your Turn

When you get sick, what do you want most?

____

____

Prayer

Jesus, thanks for being a friend to the sick. Your love reaches out to everybody. Amen.

DR. JESUS

People sometimes called Jesus "Teacher" or "Master." This puzzle will show you another name you might use for Jesus. Look up each passage about Jesus making people well. In each set of blanks, write the part of the body that Jesus made well. (The last story has two sets of blanks and two body parts.) The letters in the boxes will show you a good name for the Savior who makes people well.

Mark 3:1-6 [ ] ___ ___ ___

Luke 18:35-43 [ ] ___ ___ ___

Luke 13:10-13 ___ [ ] ___ ___

John 5:1-8 [ ] ___ ___ ___

Mark 7:33-35 ___ ___ ___ ___ ___ [ ]

___ ___ [ ] ___

(The solution is on page 249.)

JESUS, THE FRIEND OF KIDS

Jesus has time for everybody, even kids.

He said to them, "Let the little children come to me, and do not hinder them, for the kingdom of God belongs to such as these."
– Mark 10:14

Make Room for the Kids

Dennis practically ran into the Sunday school classroom. He opened his Bible and laid it on the table.

"I found such a great story," he said. "You gotta hear this story."

Mr. Kord, the Sunday school teacher, smiled and said, "You'd better tell us the story before you burst."

"Okay," Dennis said, rubbing his hands together. "Jesus is out one day teaching. There are whole families there, kids and everybody. They're all listening, and then I guess Jesus takes a break or something."

Dennis looked in his Bible before he went on.

"So some of the kids want to see Jesus. Their parents bring them so the kids can meet Him, and so He can bless the kids. But the disciples are hanging around and they're acting like bodyguards. They're like, 'Hey, get those kids out of here.'"

Dennis made his voice low and tough, and everybody laughed.

"No, really," Dennis said. "The disciples are like, 'We're big stuff and we can hang with the Master, but those kids are just a waste of time.'"

"Now here's the best part," Dennis said. "Jesus sees what's going on. You know, how the disciples are pushing the kids to the back of the line. And Jesus says, 'Don't run those kids off! You bring them over here to me. Kids are exactly the kind of people God cares about, the kind of people I came for.'"

Somebody asked, "Mr. Kord, is that the real story?"

Mr. Kord laughed and said, "Colorful, but pretty close."

Dennis said, "It makes you proud to be a kid, doesn't it?"

Your Turn

How does it make you feel to know that you are important to Jesus?

____

____

Prayer

Jesus, I know You always have time for me. The world doesn't care much about kids, but You do. Thanks for loving us all. Amen.

ADULTS ONLY?

You might think the stories in the Bible are all about grown-up servants of God. No way! There are plenty of kids who served God, too. How many of these kids do you know? See if you can match the kid on the left with what he or she did on the right. You can look up the Bible passages if you need some help.

Boy with a sack lunch (John 6:1-11)	Sang praises to Jesus
David (1 Samuel 17:41-49)	Helped feed 5,000 people
Jesus (Luke 2:41-47)	She guarded her little brother on the river
Samuel (1 Samuel 3:2-9)	Became king when seven years old
Miriam (Exodus 2:1-4)	He heard God's voice in the night
Joash (2 Kings 11:21)	Talked with the wise men in the temple
Children of Jerusalem (Matthew 21:15)	He killed a giant

(The solution is on page 249.)

JESUS, THE FIRST AND THE LAST

Jesus is Lord of everything.

"I'm A to Z, the First and the Final, Beginning and Conclusion."

– Revelation 22:13

THE MESSAGE

Jesus Has It All

As Jimmy and Duncan entered the mall, they noticed the sign over the entrance: FROM A TO Z – THIS MALL HAS IT ALL!

"That's so bogus," Jimmy said. "There's stuff you can't get at this mall."

"No joke," Duncan laughed. "You mean they don't sell kangaroos here?"

"Well, they shouldn't say it if it's not true," Jimmy argued.

"Come on, Jimmy," Duncan said. "Nobody could really have everything."

"Jesus has everything!" Jimmy said with a triumphant smile. "In the Bible Jesus says, 'I'm A to Z.'"

"What does that mean?" Duncan asked.

"That means Jesus is the Lord over the whole world from A to Z and everything in between," Jimmy said. "There's nothing in life that Jesus can't help us with. He can give us everything we need."

"So Jesus will give me a kangaroo if I ask for one?" Duncan asked. "Cool! I want a white one."

"Sure, Jesus could give you a kangaroo," Jimmy said, "except you don't really need a kangaroo. Your family lives in an apartment. Where would you keep it? How could you afford to feed it? If Jesus gave you a kangaroo it would be bad for you and even worse for the kangaroo."

"Never mind the kangaroo," Duncan said, throwing his hands in the air. "I have a great idea! Let's paint a sign over the church door: FROM A TO Z – JESUS HAS IT ALL! What do you think?"

Jimmy grinned and slapped Duncan on the back.

"I think Pastor Drake is going to love it!" Jimmy said.

Your Turn

Does Jesus care about stuff that's not religious? Why or why not?

___

___

Prayer

Jesus, there's nothing too big or too hard for You. Zilch! Zero! Nada! Nothing in the whole world! When I need help, I know whom to ask. Amen.

A TO Z AND IN BETWEEN

Every good thing in your life is a gift from Jesus. Everything that blesses you and makes you happy comes from Christ. Make an A-B-C prayer to say thank You to Him. For each letter of the alphabet, think of something for which you're grateful. Do you love hamburgers? Put that beside H. Is soccer your favorite sport? That takes care of S. You might have to get creative for some of these letters, but do your best. A is done for you, but all the rest are up to you. When you finish, read your A-B-C prayer out loud to Jesus.

A - All thanks to Jesus for:

B____________________

C____________________

D____________________

E____________________

F____________________

G____________________

H____________________

I____________________

J____________________

K____________________

L____________________

M____________________

N____________________

O____________________

P____________________

Q____________________

R____________________

S____________________

T____________________

U____________________

V____________________

W____________________

X____________________

Y____________________

Z____________________

SKY-HIGH
LOVE

MY FATHER'S WORLD

I see God's glory in what He has made.

The heavens declare the glory of God; the skies proclaim the work of his hands.

– Psalm 19:1

A Message in the Sky

The campfire had burned to a heap of coals when Counselor Dean said, "All right, it's time for our evening Bible study. Who has their Bibles with them?"

Randy raised his hand along with a couple of other boys.

"But it's too dark to read," Randy said. "Do you want me to throw some more wood on the fire?"

"No," said Dean. "Just look up and tell me what you see."

The boys tilted back their heads.

"All I see is the sky and a bunch of stars," Randy said.

"Yeah," Woody agreed. "I don't see anything about God written up there."

The other boys laughed, but Dean said, "Are you sure?"

From memory Dean recited the opening verses of Psalm 19 while the boys listened and studied the sky.

When he finished, he asked, "If you heard a really great song on the radio, wouldn't you want to know who recorded it?"

The boys nodded.

"And if you saw a beautiful picture in a museum, you'd probably want to find out who painted it," said Dean. "Great songs and paintings don't just happen by accident. Somebody has to make them."

The longer Randy stared into the sky, the more stars seemed to appear.

"When you see the stars spreading across the sky, you have to wonder who made all of it," Dean said. "The greatness of the universe tells us about the greatness of the one who made the universe. The stars talk about God without using words."

"What do they say about God?" Randy asked.

Dean answered, "The stars say, 'An awesome God made all of this!'"

Your Turn

What things in nature make you think of God?

___

___

Prayer

God, I'm amazed at all You've made! You are the biggest and the best! Amen.

AWESOME, FANTABULOUS, AMAZING GOD!

God is awesome! God is incredible! God is… Well, you know what we're getting at. What words do you use to describe our glorious God? Help the stars declare God's glory. Fill in the blanks with words that tell how super God is. If you run out of blanks before you run out of words, draw more stars!

MY FATHER'S WORLD

God rules the world.

My own hand laid the foundations of the earth, and my right hand spread out the heavens; when I summon them, they all stand up together.

– Isaiah 48:13

The Big Boss

Counselor Dean and the campers put their sleeping bags on the grass.

"What's the brightest thing in the sky tonight?" asked Dean.

"The moon," Randy said along with several other voices.

"Right," said Dean, "and the moon circles around the earth. What would happen if the moon got too close to the earth?"

"It might crash into us?" Randy guessed.

"That's right," Dean said. "What would happen if the moon got too far away?"

"It would break loose and fly into space," Gerald said.

"Right again," Dean said. "The moon circles the earth, and the earth circles the sun. What would happen if the earth got too close to the sun?"

"We'd all burn up," said Gerald, "or too far away and we'd freeze."

"Either way, we'd all be dead," Dean said. "Now find the second brightest thing in the sky."

After a few minutes of searching, Randy said, "I think it's that star over there."

"That's the planet Venus," Dean agreed. "It circles the sun, too, with earth and the other planets. Most of those planets have moons traveling around them."

"Wow!" Dean said. "All those planets and moons circle around without crashing into each other."

"Who do you think is in charge of keeping all those worlds in place and moving at the right speed?" Dean asked.

"God!" yelled several voices at once.

"You've got it," Dean said. "Remember this: if God can handle all the stars and the worlds in the universe, then God can handle anything!"

Your Turn

Is God too busy taking care of the stars to watch over you? Why or why not?

____

____

Prayer

God, I love the way You keep everything working the way it should. I know You can make my life work right, too. Amen.

KING OF THE HILL...AND EVERYTHING ELSE!

God is the biggest and best, the highest and the holiest. Some of the words describing God below are from the Bible; some are definitely not! But all of these words can remind you of the powerful God who loves you. Can you fill all these names and titles into the crossword squares?

RULER
KING
LEADER
ALMIGHTY
CHIEF
MONARCH
HEAD
BOSS
EL JEFE
MOST HIGH
LORD
CREATOR
SOVEREIGN

(The solution is on page 250.)

MY FATHER'S WORLD

Everything God made, God loves.

He determines the number of the stars
and calls them each by name.

– Psalm 147:4

Naming the Stars

"Bible study time," announced Counselor Dean.

The boys in Cabin 8 rushed outside and lay down on the grass so they could look into the starry sky.

"Let's count the stars tonight," suggested Woody.

"That might take a while," Dean said. "There are millions and billions of stars. Nobody really knows how many there are."

"Nobody knows?" asked Randy. "Are you sure about that?"

"Okay, you got me," Dean said, laughing. "God knows exactly how many stars there are. In fact, God calls each star by name."

"God gave names to all the stars?" Woody asked. "Why?"

"I think you can figure that out," Dean said. "Remember the minnows we saw in the lake today? Did you give names to them?"

"No," Woody said.

"What about your pets?" Dean asked. "Do they have names?"

"Sure," said Woody. "My dog is named Bailey and my cat is Gracie."

"I have a rabbit named Tools," Randy said, and several other boys told about their pets, too.

"Randy, how come you named your pet rabbit," Dean asked, "but we didn't name the rabbit we saw in the meadow today?"

Randy said, "I love my rabbit. I guess we give names to the things we love."

"That's right," Dean said. "So why did God name the stars?"

"Because God loves the stars," Woody said.

"Billions of stars," said Dean, "and God loves every one of them. The whole universe is wrapped in God's love. God made everything and God loves everything–even you guys!"

Your Turn

If God knows every star in the sky, how do you think God feels about people?

___

___

Prayer

God, Your love is so big that I can't imagine it. But I can sure feel it! Amen.

A WHOLE LOTTA LOVE

God loves everything in creation and that includes you. If God had a refrigerator, your picture would be stuck up there with a magnet. If God had a wallet, your photograph would be in there. Is that hard for you to believe? Here are some Bible verses to convince you. Write your name in each blank. How great does that make you feel?

Then God said, "Let us make ________________ in our image, in our likeness." (Genesis 1:26)

When I consider your heavens, the work of your fingers, the moon and the stars, which you have set in place, what is man that you are mindful of him, the son of man that you care for him? You made ________________ a little lower than the heavenly beings and crowned ________________ with glory and honor. (Psalm 8:3-5)

________________ will call upon me, and I will answer him; I will be with ________________ in trouble, I will deliver ________________ and honor ________________. (Psalm 91:15)

Who shall separate ________________ from the love of Christ? Shall trouble or hardship or persecution or famine or nakedness or danger or sword? No, in all these things we are more than conquerors through him who loved us. For I am convinced that neither death nor life, neither angels nor demons, neither the present nor the future, nor any powers, neither height nor depth, nor anything else in all creation, will be able to separate ________________ from the love of God that is in Christ Jesus our Lord. (Romans 8:35, 37-39)

Do you not know that ________________ is a temple of the Holy Spirit? (1 Corinthians 6:19)

MY FATHER'S WORLD

God gives us what we need.

He covers the sky with clouds; he supplies the earth with rain and makes grass grow on the hills. He provides food for the cattle and for the young ravens when they call.

– Psalm 147:8-9

Rainy Day God

The boys in Cabin 8 were bored.

"I'm tired of sitting in this cabin," Griffin said. "If God loves us so much, why did God send the rain to mess up this day?"

"The rain proves God loves us," Counselor Dean said. "Everybody get your rain gear on. We're taking a hike."

The boys followed Dean through the dripping woods, and to the top of a grassy hill. They could see farms in the distance.

"I wanted you to see this," Dean said.

"Wet grass," Griffin said with a dull voice. "Wow, I'm so impressed."

"Nah, open your eyes," Dean said. "Something important is happening."

The boys gazed around the meadow. They looked at each other and shrugged.

"Don't you see it?" Dean asked. "The grass is growing."

"Big duh," Griffin said.

"God is saving the world right now," Dean said. "Without the rain the grass would die. Without the grass, the mice and insects who live here would die next, and then the birds who feed on them."

Dean pointed to cattle grazing in distant fields.

"No grass, no cows," Dean said. "No cows means no hamburgers, no ice cream, no milk on your cereal."

Dean held out his hands to feel the rain on his palms.

"Without rain the world ends. It's that simple," Dean said. "Every raindrop is a reminder that God is taking care of us."

Griffin looked into the cloudy sky and let the rain patter over his face. He opened his mouth to catch the cool drops. The rain tasted like love.

Your Turn

Besides rain, how else does God take care of living things?

___

___

Prayer

God, I love You whether the sun is shining or the rain is falling. Amen.

GOD'S GIANT FRIDGE

Whether you're scarfing down burgers and fries at your favorite fast-food joint or eating carrot casserole at Aunt Petunia's house, every bite is a gift from God. And you're not the only one for whom God cares. God feeds every living creature. The whole world is like God's giant fridge where everyone can chow down. Try to match each creature below with the meal God provides.

(The solution is on page 250.)

WHAT A MIGHTY GOD!

God is stronger than anything else.

His lightning lights up the world; the earth sees and trembles.
– Psalm 97:4

Thunder and Lightning

Counselor Dean and the boys from Cabin 8 stood on a hilltop and watched the falling rain. Thunder rumbled. Suddenly a jagged fork of lightning tore across the sky. Everything grew bright for a brief moment. The thunder boomed again.

Dean rubbed his hands together in delight.

"I love storms," he said. "Just think about all the power in those clouds."

Another bolt of lightning flickered miles away.

"I took a college class where we studied the weather," Dean said. "Right now there are probably three or four thousand thunderstorms scattered in different parts of the world."

The wind grew stronger and rain splattered harder.

"Now count to 10 slowly," Dean said. "In that 10 seconds about a thousand bolts of lightning burned across the sky around the world. Who's good at math? Can you figure out how many bolts of lightning will happen today?"

Randy tried to multiply the numbers in his head, but he got lost.

Woody said, "That's over 8 million lightning bolts."

"Right," Dean said. "God sends 8 million lightning bolts every day. One lightning bolt has enough energy to power a large city for a whole year."

The lightning struck closer and the thunder made the ground shake.

"Okay, it's time to head for the cabin," Dean said. "There's too much lightning for us to stay on this hill."

Back at the cabin the boys toweled off and changed into dry clothes.

"God sure is powerful," Randy said.

"There's nothing too difficult for God," Dean said. "Nothing at all."

Your Turn

Can you think of times when God has helped you?

____

____

Prayer

God, You are awesome, mighty and powerful. I'm so glad You're my friend. Amen.

BIGGER THAN THE STORM

God shares his great power with you to help you live a great life. One reason the apostle Paul did such great things for Jesus was because he received so much power from God. If you can figure out this word box, you'll see what Paul had to say about God's power in his life.

Begin with the circled letter and connect the letters one at a time. Each letter is next to the one before—either above, below or diagonal. When you get to the period, you're finished. If you need help, you can look at Philippians 4:13.

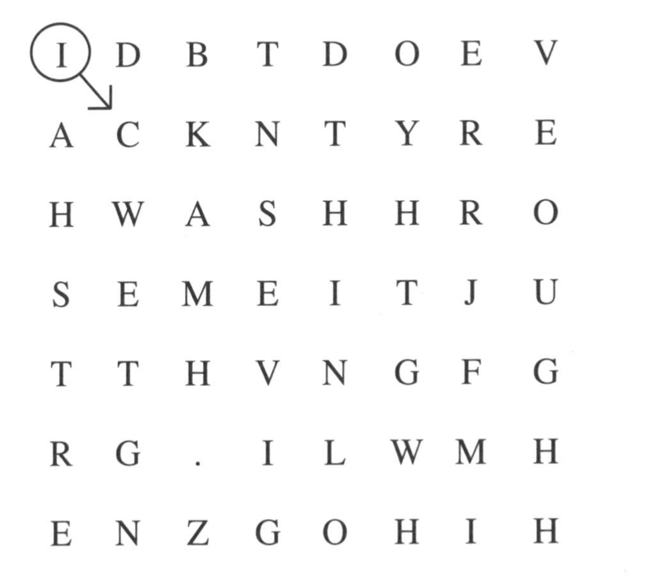

I	D	B	T	D	O	E	V
A	C	K	N	T	Y	R	E
H	W	A	S	H	H	R	O
S	E	M	E	I	T	J	U
T	T	H	V	N	G	F	G
R	G	.	I	L	W	M	H
E	N	Z	G	O	H	I	H

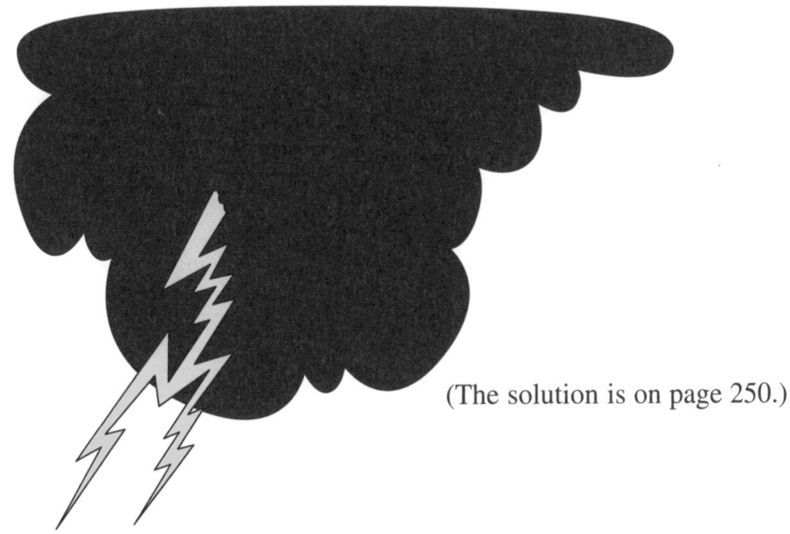

(The solution is on page 250.)

WHAT A MIGHTY GOD!

God watches over His whole creation.

The day is yours, and yours also is the night; you established the sun and moon.

– Psalm 74:16

The World's Biggest Ribbon

"The rain has finally stopped," Randy said to his friends in Cabin 8.

The campers tumbled out of the cabin, and Counselor Dean followed.

"Yea!" Gerald shouted. "That sunshine feels good!"

"Look," Woody said, "there's a rainbow."

"I know the story of the rainbow," Randy said. "At the end of the big flood after Noah got off the boat, God put the rainbow in the sky."

"Do you know why?" Dean asked.

"Not exactly," Randy said.

"The rainbow is God's promise to take care of the world," Dean said. "The rainbow means God will make the night follow the day and keep the seasons in order."

"The world would be a mess if God didn't keep everything running right," Woody said.

"Yeah, we might have winter all year long," Gerald said.

"Or it might be night all the time," Randy said. "Then the crops wouldn't grow."

"God keeps the days and seasons in order because God loves us," Dean said. "We know God is mighty in power. Let's not forget that God is also mighty in love."

"God sure went to a lot of trouble to make a safe place for us to live," Woody said.

"The world is God's gift to us, a good gift to keep us fed and happy," Dean told them.

"The rainbow reminds me of a bright ribbon," Randy said. "Maybe God wrapped the world in a rainbow ribbon so we'll remember the earth is a gift."

Your Turn

What would happen to the world if we stopped taking care of it?

___

___

Prayer

God, thank You for a wonderful world. It's a great place to live, and I'm not going to trash it up. Amen.

RAINBOW BLESSINGS

The rainbow reminds us of God's good gifts to us. Fill in each blank beside this rainbow with one of God's gifts of that color. Indigo has been done for you. Have fun with the rest! It's okay if you want to put three or four things beside some colors.

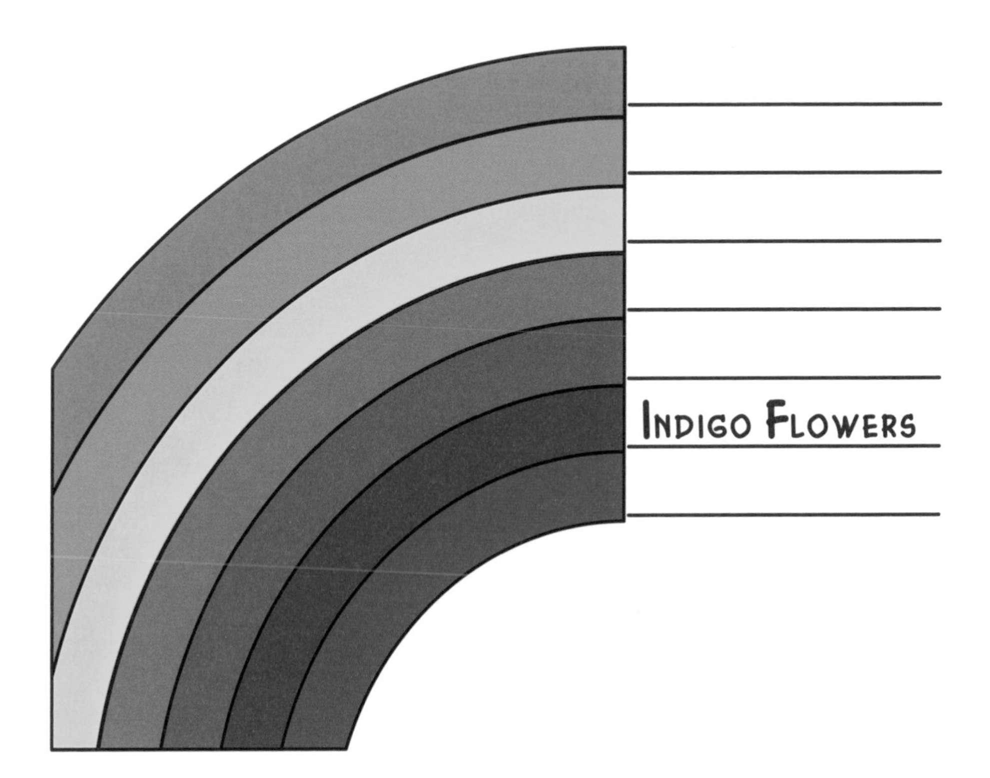

A wonderful God deserves wonderful praise.

From the rising of the sun to the place where it sets,
the name of the Lord is to be praised.

– Psalm 113:3

Sunrise, Sunset

Counselor Dean and the campers from Cabin 8 sat beside the lake watching the sun sink low in the sky. The red and orange sky reflected in the water, and a gentle breeze rippled the surface of the lake. A flock of geese landed on the lake, honking and splashing.

"When I see a beautiful sight like that," Dean said, "I feel like praising God."

"I feel a little sad," Randy said. "I love it here at camp, and now another day's ending."

"Don't forget that another day's beginning, too," Dean said.

"It doesn't look like it to me," Griffin said.

"The earth is a big ball turning in space," Dean said. "When the sun is going down here, the sun is coming up on the other side of the world."

"So, when we're saying our bedtime prayers tonight," Woody said, "somebody is saying their morning prayers."

"Awesome," Griffin said. "That means God is worshipped 24/7. When we're sleeping, somebody else is praising God, and when they're asleep we can take over."

"Like a relay race," Randy said. "We all take turns praising God."

"That's exactly how it should be," Dean said. "Our God is so incredible that the praising should never stop. Just look at this world God has made! Think of how much God loves us and all the ways God takes care of us."

"That's why the Bible says we should praise God from the rising of the sun to the setting of the sun," Randy said.

"And that means always," Griffin said.

"When God stops being wonderful, we can stop praising God," Dean said. "And that's never going to happen!"

Your Turn

Write down three wonderful things about God.

____

____

Prayer

God, I want to praise You forever! Amen.

HALLELUJAH

If people all over the world are praising God right now, then they must be praising in many languages. Did you realize you already know how to say "Praise the Lord" in Hebrew? It's "Hallelujah"!

Here's your chance to learn some new ways to say, "Praise the Lord." Try reading these aloud and see how they feel on your tongue. If you have a globe or an atlas, find each country and point to it as you say its language.

Holland (Dutch):	Prijs de here! (prayz deh heer)
France (French):	Louez l'eternel! (LOO-ay lay-ter-NEL)
Mexico (Spanish):	¡Alabado sea el señor! (ah-la-BAH-tho SAY-ah el say-NYOR)
Romania (Romanian):	Laudati pe domnul! (LAW-dah-tee pay DOME-nool)
Germany (German):	Lobt den herrn! (lohbt den hairn)
Haiti (Creole):	Lwanj pou seyè a! (l'wahj poo SAY-yay ah)
Greece (Greek):	ainete ton kurion (high-NAY-tay tahn KOO-ree-ahn)
USA (English):	Praise the Lord!

I can praise God with my whole life.

Praise him, sun and moon, praise him, all you shining stars.
– Psalm 148:3

Stars and Crickets

"How high is the sky?" Counselor Dean asked.

Dean and the boys in Cabin 8 were on a night hike, moving along the path without flashlights. The tree branches had opened overhead and the starry sky was spread above them.

"The stars are millions and millions of miles away," Randy said, "so the sky must be even higher than that."

"Good thinking," Dean said. "Now tell me what's higher than the sky."

"Is this a riddle?" Woody asked.

Dean laughed and said, "No, this is a Bible study."

"Then the answer must be God," Griffin said.

"That's right," Dean said. "The Bible teaches that God is the highest of all. God is lifted up above the sky. Even the sun, moon and stars give praise to Him."

"I thought praising God meant singing hymns or something," Griffin said. "How do stars sing?"

"Sure, singing is one way to praise God," Dean said, "but there's a better way. A star praises God by shining and following the right path through the sky."

"I don't get it," Woody said.

"Hear those crickets?" Dean said. "They rub their legs to make music in the night. That's how God made them. When crickets do what God made them for, they are praising God."

"So when we live the way God wants us to, we are praising God," Randy said.

"Right," said Dean. "When we do what God wants, then He is praised."

"What did God create us to do?" asked Griffin.

"Try to figure that out on your own," said Dean. "If you can't get it, I'll tell you tomorrow night."

Your Turn

Think of one thing you can do today that will give praise to God.

____

____

Prayer

God, today I'm going to be the best me I can be. That's the praise I want to give You! Amen.

PRAISE GOD WITH A TENNIS RACQUET

If you are a good runner, then running well is one way for you to praise God. If you are a good singer, then your singing praises God. The things we enjoy and the things we do well are gifts, and God loves to see us use our gifts.

Think about your hobbies and talents. What do you do well? What do you love doing? When you do those things, you are glorifying God.

For each letter below, fill in something you do that praises God. For example, for M you might write "Music" or for Y you could put "Youth Group." Try to fill in every blank!

M____________________________________

Y____________________________________

P____________________________________

R____________________________________

A____________________________________

I____________________________________

S____________________________________

E____________________________________

LOVE FROM ABOVE

God made me for love.

For great is your love, higher than the heavens.

– Psalm 108:4

The Simple Answer

The campers from Cabin 8 lay on their backs studying the stars above them. A shooting star flashed across the sky. The night was noisy with crickets and frogs. An owl hooted nearby, and in the distance another owl answered.

"So, have you guys figured out what God made us for?" Counselor Dean asked. "What does God want us to do with our lives?"

"We're here to make lots of money," Griffin said.

Everybody laughed.

"No," Randy said, "God put us here to watch television."

There was more laughter.

"We're here to eat!" Woody said.

"The reason we're here is to buy cool tennis shoes," another voice said.

"Our purpose in life is to get a driver's license," somebody else insisted.

"No," Dean said, chuckling. "I think your purpose is to drive me crazy, and you're doing a great job."

After the laughing stopped, Dean said, "Of all the things God does, the one thing God does best is love. The Bible says God's love is higher than the sky."

The boys looked at the distant stars and thought about how much love it would take to reach higher than the sky.

"God put us here," Dean said, "so God could love us and so we could love God and each other."

"When we love others, we're praising God?" Randy asked.

"That's right. The more you love, the more you become who God meant you to be," Dean said. "And the more you do that, the more you praise God."

"That's simple," Griffin said.

"Love is simple," Dean said, "but it's not always easy."

Your Turn

What does love mean to you?

____

____

Prayer

God, some people think love is mushy stuff, but Your love is the strongest thing of all. Give me strong love like Yours. Amen.

THE NEW COMMANDMENT

On His last night with the disciples before He was crucified, Jesus gave them a new commandment to follow forever. What was this new commandment? Decipher the code and you'll know what Jesus told His followers.

! = A	@ = C	# = D	$ = E
% = H	^ = I	& = L	* = O
+ = R	< = S	> = T	? = U
[= V	] = Y		

__________ __________

& * [$ $! @ %

__________ _____ _____

* > % $ +   ! <   ^

__________ __________

% ! [$ & * [$ #

____

] * ?

(The solution is on page 250.)

LOVE FROM ABOVE

God made the world so good because God loves me.

God alone stretched out the sky, stepped on the sea, and set the stars in place—the Big Dipper and Orion, the Pleiades and the stars in the southern sky.

– Job 9:8-9 CEV

Pictures in the Sky

"See those three bright stars in a line?" Counselor Dean asked the campers from Cabin 8. "Those make Orion's belt."

Randy said, "I see them! And there's his arm and his bow."

"Close to Orion the hunter is his faithful dog," Dean said. "Do you see the Dog Star?"

"I don't see a thing," said Griffin, "except a bunch of stars scattered around like scrambled eggs."

"Let's try another one," Dean said. "Who can find the Little Dipper?"

"That's easy," Woody said. "There it is."

"Good," Dean said. "And those two bright stars on the cup of the Dipper point straight to the North Star."

"Way cool," Woody said.

"I can't see the Dipper," Griffin complained. "The stars all look alike."

"Did God really put pictures in the sky," asked Randy, "or did people just imagine them?"

"Maybe God put so many stars in the sky just so we could enjoy looking for pictures," Dean said. "After all, God didn't have to make the world so beautiful. God could have gotten by with just 10 or 15 stars, right?"

"I'd be able to find the pictures," Griffin said. "At least a triangle or something."

"God made the world beautiful so we'd enjoy living here," Dean said. "What if God hadn't invented kangaroos? Or colors? Or fireflies? We'd get by, but the world wouldn't be nearly as much fun."

"We're God's children," Randy said, "and God wants us to have the best."

Your Turn

What have you seen this week to remind you of how wonderful the world is?

____

____

Prayer

God, the world is a great place to live. Thanks for all the wonderful things You put here for us to enjoy. Amen.

EYES TO THE SKIES

The stars can't tell the future as some people believe, but the beauty of the skies can tell you something about the Creator. Starting with the largest star, follow the star trail to read the message.

(The solution is on page 250.)

LOVE FROM ABOVE

Reminders of God are everywhere.

The whole earth is full of his glory.

– Isaiah 6:3

Look Up, Look Down

The group from Cabin 8 had hiked to the hilltop after dark for stargazing. This was their last night of camp. Tomorrow they'd be returning to their homes. Everyone felt sad knowing that their week together was ending.

"I'll miss our night-sky Bible lessons," Randy said.

"Me, too," Woody said. "I've learned a lot about God and the sky."

"When I look at the stars I'm going to think of God now," said Griffin.

"That's great," said Dean, their cabin counselor. "But you don't have to look into the sky to see God's glory. You can look anyplace and see God's work. I'll bet each of you can think of something that reminds you of God."

After a few minutes of thinking, Randy said, "There's a huge oak tree behind my house. The shade from that tree cools our whole back yard. Maybe that's a reminder of how God watches over us."

"Excellent!" Dean said.

"I miss my dog," Griffin said. "Boomer's always so glad to see me. He loves me no matter what mood I'm in. Boomer makes me think of how much God loves me. You don't think God minds being compared to Boomer, do you?"

"I don't think God minds at all," Dean said. "After all, dogs were God's idea."

The other boys mentioned places and things that made them think of God. Then Woody said, "I have a neighbor, Mr. Tyler, who is the kindest person I ever met. He's always doing something nice for somebody. He helped me get an A on my science project. When I see Mr. Tyler's smile, I think I see some of God's glory."

"Do you see what I mean?" Dean asked. "Reminders of God's goodness are everywhere if we open our eyes to find them. God is just as close at home as at summer camp."

Your Turn

Name some people you know who remind you of God's love and goodness.

____

____

Prayer

God, You are all around me, but I don't always notice. Give me eyes to see Your glory wherever I look. Amen.

HOLY HUNTING

It's time for a treasure hunt in your home. Find something in each room that reminds you of God's love and goodness. Maybe the fridge reminds you of how God feeds you. Or the bathtub might make you think of how Jesus washed you clean of sin. Carry your book through your home and write your ideas below. Look at things in a new way, and look for God everywhere!

ROOM:____________________

WHAT I FOUND:____________________

HOW IT REMINDS ME OF GOD:____________________

____

ROOM:____________________

WHAT I FOUND:____________________

HOW IT REMINDS ME OF GOD:____________________

____

ROOM:____________________

WHAT I FOUND:____________________

HOW IT REMINDS ME OF GOD:____________________

____

ROOM:____________________

WHAT I FOUND:____________________

HOW IT REMINDS ME OF GOD:____________________

____

With Jesus, every day is a new day.

"I am...the bright Morning star."

– Revelation 22:16

Follow That Star!

"Thanks for getting up so early, guys," Counselor Dean told the boys from Cabin 8. "This is our last morning at camp and I wanted to show you one more sky lesson before you go home."

"Oh, this isn't early," Griffin grumbled. "I always get up while it's still dark."

"Is it time for breakfast yet?" Woody asked.

The sky in the east was just beginning to lighten from black to gray. Dean pointed in that direction.

"See that bright star near the horizon?" he asked. "The Bible calls that the morning star. Can you guess why?"

"Maybe it gets up early, too," said Randy, yawning.

"When you see that star low in the eastern sky," Dean explained, "you know dawn is coming. The morning star is a promise that the day is about to begin."

The boys watched the morning star. Slowly the sky behind it began to turn pink, then brighter orange. As the sun rose and the sky grew brighter, other stars faded from view. Soon the morning star was the only star left in the sky.

"Jesus said, 'I am the bright Morning star,'" Dean told the boys. "That's because Jesus gives us new beginnings. With Jesus, every day is a fresh start. His love makes every day new."

The boys watched the sun rise until even the morning star faded away.

"Is the morning star gone?" Dean asked.

"No," said Randy, "it's still there. We just can't see it right now."

"Jesus is like that, too," Dean said. "We may not always be able to tell that Jesus is near, but He is there with us anyway."

"His faithfulness reaches higher than the clouds," Randy said.

"Amen," said Dean. "Now how about some pancakes?"

Your Turn

Do you worry about things in the past? Like what?

____

____

Prayer

Lord, I'm so glad You let me start over again and again. I'll try to do better today than I did yesterday, but I know You'll love me no matter what. Amen.

BRAND NEW

The Apostle Paul was once Jesus' enemy. He traveled around capturing Christians, locking them up and even helping to kill them. When Paul became a Christian, his whole life started fresh. Jesus forgave Paul his past mistakes and gave him a new beginning. Jesus does the same for you.

Here is what Paul said about getting a fresh start in Jesus. But some of the wrong words have gotten into Paul's message. To find out what Paul really said, cross out each red word and write its opposite above it.

Therefore, if **no one** is in Christ,

he is a **old destruction**;

the **new** has gone,

the **old** has come!

(The solution is on page 250.)

MAKING A
BETTER WORLD

BEING A FRIEND

God wants me to be brothers and sisters with others.

Whoever welcomes one of these little children in my name welcomes me.

– Mark 9:37

The Big Brother

Robbie stood on the sidewalk. He bounced the basketball, glancing up and down the street. He looked at his watch and continued dribbling the ball.

He knew Frank would come soon. Frank and Robbie had been getting together for four years. Sometimes they went out for pizza or saw a movie. All that really mattered to Robbie was spending time together.

Robbie was very young when his father died. Robbie's mother was great, but sometimes Robbie just wanted an older guy to hang out with. There was some stuff he didn't want to talk about with his mom.

Frank was Robbie's big brother. Frank wasn't really related to Robbie, but once a week Frank hung out with Robbie.

Robbie heard the rattle of Frank's old car chugging up the street. Frank pulled over to the curb.

"Hey, Rob-o!" Frank yelled. "Let's go have some fun."

As they drove toward the park, Robbie said, "I've been thinking."

"I thought I smelled something smoking," Frank said.

"Har-har!" Robbie said. "Do you think I could be a big brother when I get older?"

"Sure," Frank said. "You'd make a super big brother. Some kid would be lucky to have you for a friend."

"Is it fun?" Robbie asked. "You know, being a big brother?"

"It's a blast!" Frank said. "Especially if you get a great little brother like I have."

"I'd like helping a kid without a dad," Robbie said. "I think I might try it some day."

Your Turn

Why do you think Robbie wanted to be a big brother?

Prayer

God, thanks for the people who care about me. People like that make my life so much better. Amen.

FRIENDS: TRUE OR FALSE

The prophet Jeremiah had a surprising friend named Ebed-Melech. Jeremiah came from Judah, and Ebed-Melech was from Ethiopia. The two men were different races. Ebed-Melech worked for the king and Jeremiah was often in trouble with the king.

In spite of their differences, Ebed-Melech was a good friend to Jeremiah. When Jewish leaders punished Jeremiah and threw him into a dry well to die, Ebed-Melech asked the king for permission to rescue Jeremiah. Ebed-Melech took some other men and they pulled Jeremiah out of the well with long ropes. Ebed-Melech even got old clothing for Jeremiah to put under his arms so the ropes wouldn't bruise him. (You can read the whole story in Jeremiah 38.)

Ebed-Melech proved himself a true friend to Jeremiah. What does it mean to be a true friend? What do you think? Here are some true-false questions to help you think about true and false friends. Circle the answer that makes the most sense to you.

True or False People can be friends even if they are quite different.

True or False Friends help each other out.

True or False Friends only come around for fun times.

True or False A friend ignores you when you're in trouble.

True or False A friend shares his life with you.

True or False People can be friends even if they disagree and fight sometimes.

True or False A friend sticks by you when other people turn against you.

True or False A friend cares about your feelings.

True or False A friend will like you only if you always do what he wants to do.

True or False A true friend is a precious treasure.

True or False I know how to be a true friend to others.

BEING A FRIEND

Friends take care of each other.

A friend is always loyal, and a brother is born to help in time of need.

– Proverbs 17:17 NLT

The Bus Buddy

The two women in the supermarket reached for the same bottle of soap at the same time. Both of them laughed. One woman held out the soap to the other and said, "Aren't you Cameron Storm's mother?"

"Yes," Mrs. Storm said.

"My son Graham Batson rides the bus with Cameron," the other woman explained quietly.

"Yes, Cameron has told me how much he likes Graham," Mrs. Storm said. "I think they swap jokes every morning."

Mrs. Batson smiled and said, "My Graham is a special child. He's mentally retarded. He's in a separate class, but he rides the bus with the other students."

"Cameron never mentioned that," Mrs. Storm said.

"Graham just loves Cameron," Mrs. Batson said. "Cameron is a little older, but he often sits with Graham on the bus. Cameron is like a big brother to my son. Graham told me the kids on the bus used to make fun of him. Now that Cameron is his friend, the others have stopped picking on Graham."

"I didn't know about any of this," Mrs. Storm said with surprise.

Mrs. Batson laid one hand on Mrs. Storm's arm.

"It means so much to us that Graham has a friend like Cameron," Mrs. Batson said. "I've never met your son, but he must be a wonderful person. The world needs more people like him."

Later that afternoon, Mrs. Storm was putting away groceries when Cameron came into the kitchen. Mrs. Storm wrapped her son in a long hug and kissed him on the forehead.

"What's that for?" Cameron asked.

"Just because I'm proud of you," his mother said.

Your Turn

What do you look for in a friend?

____

____

Prayer

God, help me be a friend to someone who really needs a friend. Amen.

WWJD?

Do you ever ask yourself, “What would Jesus do if He were in my place?” If you’re wondering how to be a friend to others, WWJD is a good place to start. Write what you think Jesus would do to be a friend to these people:

A boy in a wheelchair watching your neighborhood basketball game.

____

____

A new girl in school who doesn’t speak English very well.

____

____

A boy who gets picked on because medical treatments have made his hair fall out.

____

____

A soccer teammate whose bad play makes your team lose the game.

____

____

A boy who is having trouble keeping up in history class.

____

____

A friend who belongs to a different religion and doesn’t understand what Christmas is.

____

____

____

Older people know a lot because they've lived a lot.

Gray hair is a crown of glory; it is gained by living a godly life.

– Proverbs 16:31 NLT

The Time Machine

"I'm going to the nursing home for a while," Iniko told his mother. "I'm going to visit with Mr. Dibny."

"I thought you didn't like 'old people,'" Iniko's mother said. "You said they're scary and boring."

"I was wrong," Iniko said. "Remember when our youth group went caroling at the nursing home? After the singing we had hot chocolate and cookies with some of the people who live there. That's when I got to know Mr. Dibny. He's awesome."

Iniko's mother smiled.

"What do you do when you visit your friend?" she asked.

"Sometimes we watch TV or play checkers," Iniko said. "Mr. Dibny is in a wheelchair and I push him around the nursing home."

"That's nice," Iniko's mother said.

"Mostly we just talk," Iniko said. "I tell him about school, and he tells me stories about the old days."

"The old days?"

"Yeah. Mr. Dibny tells me about the Depression and World War II and all kinds of stuff," Iniko said. "He can remember before there was television and he wore button-up shoes when he was a boy. He used to have a car that he had to crank with a handle to get it started."

"I guess Mr. Dibny is like a time machine for you," Iniko's mother said. "When he tells you those stories you get to go back in time."

"It does feel like going back to the old days," Iniko said. "But Mr. Dibny isn't my time machine. He's my friend."

Your Turn

Besides people in your family, do you have any friends who have lived a long time? What do you think of them?

____

____

Prayer

God, could You help me find some friends who have been around for a long time? I think gray hair is cool. Amen.

MAKE YOUR OWN TIME MACHINE

How would you like to travel into the past? It's easy with a timeline. Divide the line below into sections, one for each year of your life so far. Write your birthdate on one end and today's date on the other end. Make marks on the line to represent important events in your life. Be sure to label each mark. You might want to mark your first day of school, your baptism or a favorite vacation. Mark enough things on your timeline so someone could study it and get an idea of what your life has been like.

When you've finished your timeline, find an older person to fill in the other timeline. Maybe a grandparent or a neighbor or a church friend would enjoy doing this. When you've finished, talk about how your lives have been alike or different. Try to make guesses about what lies ahead on your timelines!

MY TIMELINE

MY FRIEND'S TIMELINE

BEING A FRIEND

God wants me to treat older people with kindness.

Rise in the presence of the aged, show respect for the elderly and revere your God.

– Leviticus 19:32

The Four-legged Visitor

Iniko led Scruffy the spaniel into the metal tub filled with soapy water. Scruffy stood very still while Iniko scrubbed him with a sponge. When Scruffy was clean, Iniko got him out of the tub and washed away the suds with the garden hose.

Iniko's mother came out of the house to watch. She said, "Iniko, we've had Scruffy for six years. Every time he needs a bath I have to make you do it, and you fuss about it the whole time. This is the first time you've ever given him a bath without my telling you to."

"I want Scruffy to look extra good," Iniko said. "I'm taking him to visit Mr. Dibny today."

"At the nursing home?" Iniko's mother asked. "Is that allowed?"

"Yeah," Iniko said. "The people at the nursing home love for pets to come visit them. Last week some lady brought a rabbit and everybody petted it."

"Scruffy is so big," Iniko's mother said.

"But he's very gentle," Iniko said. "He doesn't bark and he likes strangers. I already asked one of the nurses at the home and she said it would be fine to bring Scruffy today."

"You'd better put him on a leash," Iniko's mother said.

"I'm going to put on the pretty red leash," Iniko said. "I'll let Mr. Dibny hold the leash while I push his wheelchair. We'll go all over the home so everybody can meet Scruffy."

Iniko's mother laughed. She rubbed the dog's head and said, "Scruffy, have a good time today, and try to get Iniko home in time for dinner."

Your Turn

Do you think older people like to have fun? Why or why not?

____

____

Prayer

God, today I'm going to help somebody have a happier day. Please show me who and how. Amen.

GRAY-HAIRED HEROES

Identify these wise and faithful people from the Bible. (If you need help, you can look up the Bible references.) Write their names on the lines.

1. I was 75 years old when God called me to go to a new land. (Genesis 12:1-4)
2. I was content to die after I met baby Jesus. (Luke 2:25-32)
3. I was 600 years old when God sent a flood and I saved my family in an ark. (Genesis 7:6-10)
4. I led the people of Israel through the wilderness and brought them to the land of God's promise. (Exodus 34:5-8)
5. I was an old woman when I gave birth to a baby named Isaac. (Genesis 18:10-15)
6. I was a prophetess who saw baby Jesus in the temple and told everyone about God's plan for saving Israel. (Luke 2:36-38)
7. I am the oldest man in the Bible. I lived 969 years! (Genesis 5:27)

1. ____________________ 2. ____________________

3. ____________________ 4. ____________________

5. ____________________ 6. ____________________

7. ____________________

(The solution is on page 250.)

God wants me to welcome newcomers.

Don't mistreat any foreigners who live in your land.

– Leviticus 19:33 CEV

The New Kid

"Here comes the new kid," Conner said.

Mark and Conner were waiting at the end of the lunch line in the cafeteria.

"Naoko is a stupid name," Mark said.

"Shhh!" Conner whispered. "Here he comes."

"It doesn't matter," Mark said. He smiled at Naoko and said, "You don't understand what we're saying, do you?"

Naoko smiled and nodded. Conner thought he looked lonely and a little scared. He thought about how he'd feel in a foreign country where he couldn't speak the language. He turned to Naoko and pointed a finger at his own chest.

"Conner," he said slowly. Then he pointed at Mark and said, "Mark."

Naoko smiled back. "Conner," he said. "Mark. Hel-lo. My name Naoko."

"Hello, Naoko," Conner said. He looked hard at his friend.

"Oh, all right," Mark said, rolling his eyes. "Hello, Naoko."

Once again Naoko said, "Hel-lo."

"Look," Mark said, "if we're going to teach him English, let's cover the important stuff."

Mark pointed to a serving tray and made a face. He said, "Cabbage. Yuck."

Naoko repeated the words. Conner and Mark laughed, and when Conner slapped Naoko on the back, the Japanese boy laughed, too.

Conner pointed to another tray.

"Pizza," Conner said. He rubbed his belly and added, "Good!"

Naoko said, "Pete-sah good." He rubbed his belly and said, "Ex-tra cheese."

Conner said, "Naoko is going to get along fine here."

"Yeah," Mark said. "He just needs a couple of friends to get started."

Naoko smiled again and said, "Good!"

Your Turn

If someone couldn't understand you, how could you be a friend to that person?

____

____

Prayer

God, when new people come to my school or move to my neighborhood, help me to welcome them. Amen.

DON'T MISS THE BLESSING!

Refugees are people who leave their homes and travel to other countries, usually to escape danger or hardship. Did you know Jesus was a refugee? When He was just a baby, Jesus' family fled from a murderous king in Israel and hid in Egypt. Jesus spent part of His boyhood as a stranger in a foreign country.

The newcomers and foreigners who enter your life might be sent by God to bring you friendship or new ideas. What if you turn them away? You might miss a blessing.

Use these clues to fill in the missing words from this Bible message about strangers.

1. Sounds like something in your shoelace
2. Sounds like what golfers yell
3. Fetch
4. Sounds like the second number
5. Come in
6. Sounds like the number after three
7. Sounds like a job done with needle and thread
8. Sounds like the answer to an addition problem
9. "Hark the herald _____"
10. The opposite of in
11. Sounds like the opposite of yes

Do _______________ _______________ _______________

_______________tain strangers, _______________ by

_______________ doing _______________ people have entertained

_______________ with _______________ _______________ing it.

(The solution is on page 250.)

Families have room for lots of love.

I was a stranger and you invited me in.

– Matthew 25:35

The Outsider

"Are you going to marry that guy?" Ethan Troy asked.

Ethan's mother stirred a bubbling pot on the stove. She lowered the heat.

"I wish you wouldn't call him 'that guy,'" said Mrs. Troy. "His name is Trevor. He's been very kind to you."

"So, are you going to marry him?" Ethan persisted. "Even if you do, he's never going to be my father."

"Trevor's not trying to be your father," said Ethan's mom, "but he'd like to be your friend."

"I've already got plenty of friends," Ethan said.

"Yes," said Mrs. Troy, "and when they come here I make them feel welcome. You should do the same for my friend Trevor."

Ethan's mom looked into the oven, then turned to Ethan.

"I know you miss your dad," she said. "So do I. But everything changes, Ethan, even families. I don't know if I'll marry Trevor, but I like spending time with him. Can't you make room for him around here?"

Ethan stared at the floor and said nothing. His mother sighed.

"I'm going to change clothes before Trevor gets here," she told Ethan.

When his mother had gone to her room, Ethan heard a car door slam. He looked outside and saw Trevor climbing the front steps. He always pretended he didn't hear the doorbell so his mom would have to let Trevor in.

The bell rang now. Ethan glanced toward his mother's bedroom door. After a minute, the bell rang again. Another minute passed.

It would be mean to leave the guy standing out there, Ethan decided. Maybe his mom was right. Maybe he should give Trevor a chance.

Ethan stared at the door and wondered what to do.

Your Turn

Have new people ever come into your family? How did that feel to you?

____

____

Prayer

God, You've put plenty of room in my heart for friends and family. Give me enough love for everybody. Amen.

MAKING ROOM

Sometimes you have to make room for new people in your life. The Bible is full of stories about people who made room for others. Abraham made room in his family for his nephew Lot. Pharaoh's daughter adopted Moses and made room for him in her home. Jacob made room in his life for 13 sons and daughters. After Jesus went back to heaven, John the disciple made room for Jesus' mother, Mary, in his life. You can do this for others because God has done this for you. Once you were an outsider, but God has loved you and welcomed you into His household.

To read what Paul says about this in Ephesians 1:5, shift each letter forward one step in the alphabet. For instance, change A to B and change Y to Z.

GD OQDCDRSHMDC TR SN AD ZCNOSDC ZR

____

GHR RNMR SGQNTFG IDRTR BGQHRS.

____

(The solution is on page 250.)

HELPING OTHERS

God wants me to help others.

Rescue the weak and needy.

– Psalm 82:4

Visiting Yard Sales

Craig coasted his bike to a stop and got off. He propped it on the kick stand and walked up the driveway. He had read about the yard sale in the newspaper. Every week Craig watched for yard sales in his neighborhood.

A woman sat in a lawn chair in the open garage. She was surrounded by tables filled with household items for sale.

"Hi," Craig said. "I'm Craig Walton. I live two blocks over."

"Hi, Craig," the woman said. "Are you shopping today?"

"Not really," Craig said.

He handed her a card with the name of his church and a phone number.

"When you finish your garage sale," Craig said, "if you have leftover stuff you don't want anymore, you can call that number and somebody from my church will come and get it."

"What will your church do with it?" asked the woman.

"We sort it and put it on shelves in the church basement," Craig explained. "When needy people ask for help, we let them take anything they can use. And we have our own flea market to buy groceries for hungry families."

"What a good thing to do," the woman said. "I'd love for your church to haul away whatever's left after my sale. I don't want it back in my house!"

"That would be great," Craig said.

"So, Craig, this is your job to visit all the yard sales in the neighborhood?" the woman asked.

"Our pastor says Christians should help make the world a better place," Craig said. "I decided I can do this and it might help a little."

The woman smiled and said, "Craig, I think I'll visit your church Sunday. It sounds like a good place."

Your Turn

Do you know any kids who are helping others? What do they do?

____

____

Prayer

God, this is a good world, but there are lots of ways it could be better. Show me what I can do to make a difference. Amen.

SHARING YOUR STUFF

Your house is probably filled with stuff you don't want or need anymore. Did you know that stuff can help other people? There are probably groups in your town who will take that stuff and give it to people who can use it or sell it to help families in need.

Ask your mom or dad to help you fill a box with unwanted stuff from around your house. When the box is full, give it away. If you don't know where to give things away, check with your pastor or look in the phone book.

Here's a checklist to help you fill that box quickly. Look for:

_____ Books you've already read

_____ CDs you're tired of

_____ Clothes you've outgrown

_____ Winter coats you don't need

_____ Gifts you didn't need or didn't like

_____ Old TVs and radios that need a little repair

_____ Old towels, sheets and blankets in good shape

_____ Toys, games and puzzles you're tired of

_____ Old furniture

_____ Kitchen stuff your parents don't use

_____ Tools your parents don't use

_____ Stuff in the garage

_____ Stuff in the attic

HELPING OTHERS

I can help neighbors I haven't even met.

Love your neighbor as yourself.

– Romans 13:9

The Youth Group Project

Diego stood up before his youth group. He didn't like speaking to groups. He felt nervous as he said, "I have an idea to talk about."

He held up a small object.

"Does everybody know what this is?" he asked.

"Sure," said Basilio. "That's the cartridge from a computer printer."

"An empty ink cartridge," Diego said. "Throw it away, right? Wrong! Recycling companies will pay money for this."

"That's cool," Xavier said.

"And I know a church group that collects these and sells them," Diego said. "They use the money to set up after-school programs for kids in the city. They help kids stay out of gangs and keep away from drugs."

"I know kids in my school who could use that kind of help," Xavier said.

"We've got a computer at my house," Basilio said. "We could bring in our old cartridges."

"My mom works in an office with a ton of computers," someone else said. "I'll bet she could get a bunch."

"We can get everybody in church to bring their old ink cases," Xavier said.

"I'll mail them whenever we get a boxful," Diego said.

"I'll make posters to hang around the church to remind people," one of the girls said.

"I can decorate a collection box to put in the hallway," offered another boy.

"Let's set a goal," said Basilio. "We'll try to get 300 cartridges this year."

"I'll put an article in the church newsletter," said Xavier, "and something in the Sunday bulletin, too."

Diego sat down. He had a smile on his face. He still didn't like talking in front of a group, but he did like helping people.

Your Turn

Why would you help people you've never met?

____

____

Prayer

Jesus, You tried to help everyone You could. I want to be a helper like You. Amen.

MAKING OLD THINGS NEW

Recycling means taking old things and making them new again. Old cans and bottles get melted and made into new containers. Old batteries get recharged. Old ink cartridges get refilled and restored.

Did you know that God is a recycler? Yep! In Revelation 21:5, God sits on the throne of heaven and He says, "I am a recycler!" Well, those aren't the exact words. To find out what God really says, hold this page up to a mirror.

(The answer is on page 250.)

HELPING OTHERS

God loves animals, too.

A righteous man cares for the needs of his animal.

– Proverbs 12:10

The Thirsty Dog

Zach was too tired to pedal his bike, so he walked it toward home.

The street was deserted because it was so hot outside. Half a block from his house, Zach saw a dog slumped in a front yard. The dog was tied to a stake and its water bowl was empty and dry. So was its food bowl.

Zach knocked on the front door of the house. After a long time, a very thin woman opened the door.

"Hi, Mrs. Rogers," Zach said. "Have you given your dog water today?"

The woman frowned and her forehead wrinkled.

"I can't remember," she said at last. "I've been sick. I haven't felt up to going outside."

"Maybe I could help," Zach said. "I live just up the street. I'd be glad to take care of your dog."

"I couldn't pay you," Mrs. Rogers said.

"That's okay," Zach said. "I don't have a dog of my own. I'd like to come see your dog every day. Where do you keep his food?"

"In the shed behind the house," Mrs. Rogers said. "There's a big bag there. His name is Bruno."

"Leave it to me," Zach said. "I'll take care of Bruno for you."

Mrs. Rogers closed her door, and Zach filled Bruno's water bowl from the hose. By the time Zach returned from the shed with food, Bruno's water bowl was empty. Zach filled it again. Bruno lapped it thirstily.

"Don't worry, Bruno," Zach said. "You won't be thirsty anymore."

Bruno looked up from the bowl and licked Zach's hand.

"You're welcome," Zach said.

Your Turn

Why should you be kind to animals?

____

____

Prayer

God, You made me and You made animals, too. Help me take care of pets the way You take care of me. Amen.

ALL GOD'S CREATURES

When God told Noah to make an ark to save his family from the flood, God made sure Noah saved the animals, too. When you think about how God made each animal different and special, you know God must love animals a lot. Just for fun, here are some animal riddles. First you have to fill in the right animal by finding that animal in the Bible passage. Then you have to figure out the answer to the riddle. The solution is on page 251.

What is the smartest kind of __________? (Deuteronomy 1:44)

Answer:

What do__________ play on the piano? (Luke 5:6)

Answer:

What do you call a crying __________? (Matthew 19:24)

Answer:

Why don't __________ drive cars? (Matthew 8:30)

Answer:

What __________ never goes out in the daylight? (Revelation 6:2)

Answer:

Why are __________ like playing cards? (Genesis 49:27)

Answer:

What do you call a sleeping __________? (1 Samuel 1:25)

Answer:

How is a __________ like a top? (Job 8:14)

Answer:

What kind of __________ has red spots? (Jeremiah 13:23)

Answer:

Which side of a __________ has the most hair? (Proverbs 26:17)

Answer:

CARING FOR GOD'S WORLD

I show my love for God by taking care of His world.

In the beginning God created the heavens and the earth.
– Genesis 1:1

Going to the Mall

"Dad, can you drive me to the mall?" Alex Nelson asked. "I want to go to the bookstore."

"Your sister has a gymnastics class near the mall tomorrow. Let's do both things on one trip," said Mr. Nelson.

"Why do I have to wait for her dumb gym class?" Alex said.

Alex's father lowered his newspaper. He said, "Alex, every time we drive the car we put pollution into the air. The mall is 10 miles away. We drive 20 miles back and forth when we go to the mall."

"Do I have to walk to the mall?" Alex asked.

Alex's father said, "I could drive you to the mall today. Then I could go back tomorrow morning to shop for groceries, and take your sister to her class tomorrow afternoon. That's three trips to the mall. Sixty miles."

"Or we could do all three things on one trip," Alex said.

"Right," said his father. "That would be only 20 miles of driving."

"And less air pollution," Alex said.

"Remember how gray the air was last week?" Mr. Nelson asked. "That's what happens when too many people drive more than they need to."

"On the news they were asking people with breathing problems to stay at home," Alex recalled.

"When we drive less, we're taking care of God's world," Alex's dad said. "So how about that book? Can you wait until tomorrow?"

"Sure, Dad," Alex said. "No problem."

Your Turn

Saving water, electricity and gasoline make a better world. Make a list of things your family can do to take care of God's world.

____

____

Prayer

God, there's enough in the world to take care of us all, but not enough to waste. Help me to use only as much as I need. Amen.

RUNNING IN CIRCLES

Sometimes people use their cars more than they need. It's easy to forget that every time you use a car you are using up fossil fuels from the earth and adding pollution to the air. People don't have to get rid of their cars, but we can use common sense and look for ways to drive less. If we do, we'll all be better off, and so will planet earth!

You need a coin and a game marker (maybe another coin) to play this game. Put your marker at Start. The object is to see how quickly you can get around the track to the Finish. You can play with a friend or you can play alone and try to beat your best record.

To play, put your marker at Start and flip the coin. For heads, you can move two spaces. For tails you can move one space. Always follow the instructions on the spot where you land. Have fun!

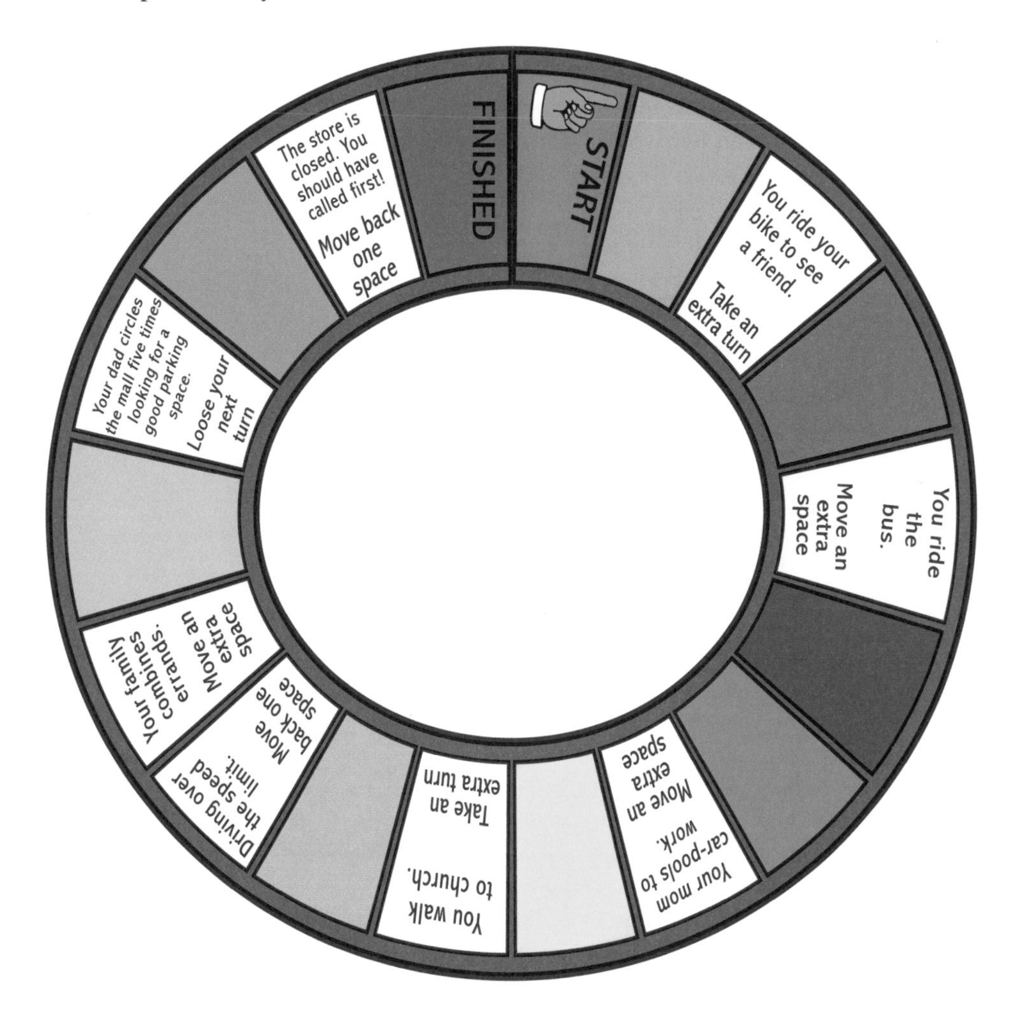

CARING FOR GOD'S WORLD

God wants me to take care of my world.

The earth is the Lord's, and everything in it, the world, and all who live in it.

– Psalm 24:1

Spring Cleaning

"Look at all this trash," Emilio said.

Emilio and his friend Kwame were helping with River Sweep, a Saturday project to pick up litter along the river. Emilio and Kwame had been sent to the park beside the river. They each wore River Sweep T-shirts.

"Some people just think the world is their garbage can," Kwame said.

He carried a stick with a nail in the end. With the stick he stabbed a paper coffee cup and put it in his trash bag.

"And it's not even our world," Emilio said. "It's God's world."

Kwame speared a fast food bag and said, "Yeah, it's God's world, and we're supposed to take care of it."

Emilio leaned over the water to snag a plastic six-pack ring.

"I'll bet it makes God sad to see what a mess we've made," Emilio said.

The boys leaned on their sticks and rested. In the park, a group of teenagers got up from a picnic table and piled into their car. They left the picnic table covered with bottles and food wrappers. The wind lifted a paper napkin and blew it along the ground.

"But I'll bet God is glad when we clean up the mess," Kwame said.

The boys looked back along the riverfront where they'd been working. The bank was clean and beautiful. Not a single piece of litter was in sight.

"I'll get the trash on the picnic table," Emilio said.

"I'll help," Kwame said. "Then let's get new trash bags. These are getting heavy."

Your Turn

What do you do when you see a piece of trash on the ground?

____

____

Prayer

God, this world is a beautiful place, and I want to keep it that way. You can count on me to put garbage where it belongs. Amen.

WHAT A WONDERFUL WORLD

Do you want to find out how God feels about the world? Read what the message wheel says (from Genesis 1:31). Start with the circled letter at the top of the wheel and move to the right. Skip the second letter, read the next one, and so on, reading every other letter all the way around the wheel. When you've gone around the wheel twice and you end up at the period, you'll have the whole message.

(The solution is on page 251.)

CARING FOR GOD'S WORLD

God made a good world.

God saw all that he had made, and it was very good.
– Genesis 1:31

Partners with God

"Mom, do we have room to plant more trees in our yard?" Ben asked.

"I think so," his mom answered. "Do we need more trees?"

"The world needs more trees, Mom," Ben answered. "We've been studying trees in science class. Did you know trees make oxygen for us to breathe?"

"Yes," Ben's mother said.

"Trees give homes and food to different animals," Ben went on. "Tree roots keep rain from washing away the dirt. Shade will make our house cooler in the summer. We can even use the leaves in our garden."

"Trees take some work," Ben's mother said. "Who's going to take care of our new trees?"

"I'll water them," Ben said. "While the trees are small, I'll pull up the grass and weeds around them. When they get big, I'll rake the leaves that fall."

Ben's mother laughed.

"All right," she said. "You've convinced me."

"Let's go buy some trees right now," Ben said.

"We don't have to buy trees," Ben's mother told him. "We can plant acorns and maple seeds this fall. By next spring they'll be growing."

"But they'll be tiny," Ben said.

"Of course," his mother said. "Did you think trees started big? But if you take care of those tiny trees, God will make them grow. In four or five years, they'll be taller than you."

"Planting trees makes the world a better place," Ben said.

"That's right," his mother agreed. "Planting trees makes us God's partners."

Your Turn

Do you think God wants your help in taking care of the world? Why or why not?

____

____

Prayer

God, I love working with You to take care of Your world. Thanks for letting me be Your partner! Amen.

ONLY GOD CAN MAKE A TREE, BUT ANYBODY CAN PLANT ONE

Is there room for more trees in your yard? How about the yard of a neighbor or relative? Or at your school or church? Of course, you must get permission before planting trees on someone else's property. Where can you get trees to plant? You might find seeds and nuts in your local park or your own neighborhood. Sometimes unwanted trees sprout in gardens or even cracks in the driveway. These can be dug up and transplanted. Some groups give away small trees to anyone who will plant them. Ask at your library or your county extension office about tree giveaways. How do you plant and care for a young tree? You can get more information at your library, but here are a few pointers:

- Plant your tree in a place where it will have plenty of room to grow. When selecting a place, imagine your tree very large and tall!
- Dig a hole, chop up the soil until it is loose and carefully plant the tree or seed.
- If you plant a seed, mark the spot with a stake so you can watch for it to come up. This may take several months or even a year. You can plant several seeds or nuts in one spot to make sure one of them sprouts, but if more than one comes up you will have to pull out all but the strongest one.
- If you plant a young tree, keep it well watered while it gets used to its new home. Watering is the most important thing you can do!
- Keep weeds and grass pulled up around the little tree.
- Young trees may need a stake to protect them from getting stepped on or run over by the lawnmower.

That's it! God will take care of the rest.

And someday your children may build a tree house in your tree!

HOLY STUFF

THE BIBLE

The Bible teaches me about Jesus.

Heaven and earth will pass away, but my words will never pass away.

– Mark 13:31

The Big Deal Book

"Everybody's always talking about how important the Bible is," Wesley complained as he and his friend Calvin walked home from youth group.

"I don't get it," Wesley said. "It's just an old book and it's hard to read."

Calvin said, "Not all of it is hard. Besides, some versions of the Bible are especially for kids, and they're easy to read."

"But there are lots of great books around," Wesley said. "What's the big deal about the Bible?"

"That's easy," Calvin said. "The Bible tells us about the most important person in the whole universe: Jesus."

"I'd rather read about Jesus in a comic book," Wesley said.

"I've got some comic books about Jesus," Calvin said. "I'll loan them to you, but they just tell the same stories as the Bible. That's because the only stories we have about Jesus come from the Bible."

"Really?" Wesley asked.

"Sure," Calvin said. "The Bible tells who Jesus was. No other book does that."

"So if we didn't have the Bible," Wesley asked, "we wouldn't know Jesus?"

"That's right," Calvin said. He reached into his backpack and pulled out a Bible. "This book tells us everything we know about Jesus."

"Now I see why the Bible is a big deal," Wesley said. "Where in the Bible are the stories about Jesus?"

"Look in the books of Matthew, Mark, Luke and John," said Calvin. They stopped under a streetlight and Calvin showed Wesley where to find those books.

"Maybe the Bible's not so hard," Wesley said.

"Maybe not," Calvin agreed.

Your Turn

What do you like about the Bible?

____

____

Prayer

Jesus, I love to read about You in the Bible. The more I read about You, the more I know about You. And the more I know about You, the more I love You. Amen.

IT'S GREEK TO ME

The Gospels–Matthew, Mark, Luke and John–are books about Jesus. The Gospels are over 1900 years old and they were written in a language called Greek.

Here is a message written in Greek letters. Use the key to figure out the message.

A = A	Ch = Ξ	D = Δ	E = E
F, Ph = Φ	I = I	M = M	N = N
O = O	R = Π	S = Σ	T = T
Th = Θ			

ΞΠΙΣΤ ΙΣ ΠΙΣΕΝ ΦΠΟΜ ΘΕ ΔΕΑΔ

___

___

(The solution is on page 251.)

The Bible teaches me how to live.

Your word is a lamp to my feet and a light for my path.

– Psalm 119:105

Learning the Rules

"This stinks," David said. He had a board game open on the table, pieces and cards spread before him. He turned the box upside down and shook it over the table.

"What's the matter?" asked his older sister, Bethany.

"I bought this game at the flea market," David explained. "I thought it looked like a lot of fun. The board is a battlefield and the pieces are little soldiers."

"So what's the problem?"

"The rules aren't in the box," David said. "How am I supposed to know how the game works without the rules?"

"So you've got a board, dice, a spinner and a bunch of pieces," Bethany said, "but you don't know how to play."

"I only paid a dollar for the game," David said, "but I still got ripped off. Without the rules none of this stuff makes sense."

"It could be worse," Bethany said. "What if we didn't have any rules for life?"

"Duh," said David. "Life doesn't have rules."

"Sure it does," Bethany told him. "The Bible gives us directions for living."

"I thought the Bible was full of boring stuff," David said.

"God invented life and gave us the Bible so we'd know how to live," Bethany said. "Without the Bible, life is just like that game. It doesn't make any sense."

Your Turn

How can the Bible help you in life?

____

____

Prayer

God, the Bible is the coolest book in the world! The more I read it, the more I understand how You want me to live. Amen.

THE BIG TWO

God gave Moses 10 rules for living. We call them the Ten Commandments. Fill in the blanks for the Ten Commandments. If you need help you can find the commandments in Exodus 20:1-17.

1. You shall have no other ______________ before me.
2. You shall not make or worship an ______________.
3. You shall not misuse God's ______________.
4. Keep the ______________ day holy.
5. Honor your ______________ and ______________.
6. You shall not ______________.
7. You shall not commit ______________.
8. You shall not ______________.
9. You shall not give false ______________.
10. You shall not ______________.

One day a man asked Jesus about the most important rules for living. Jesus gave the man two rules. Jesus said these two rules are big enough to cover all the others. Fill in the blanks. If you need help, you can read the whole story in Mark 12:28-34.

Rule 1: Love the Lord your God with all your ____________ and with all your _________ and with all your __________ and with all your _________.

Rule 2: Love your ____________ as ___________.

(The solution is on page 251.)

God talks to me through the Bible.

Everything in the Scriptures is God's Word.

– 2 Timothy 3:16 CEV

The Letter

Brad Danvers took the frame from the wall and handed it carefully to his friend James.

"Wow, that is so cool," James said.

"My dad is real proud of it," Brad said.

In the frame was a typed letter on White House stationery signed by President Jimmy Carter.

"When dad was a boy he wrote a letter to President Carter," Brad said, "and the President wrote back."

Just then, Brad's dad walked in.

"I was so excited that the President wrote back to me," Mr. Danvers explained. "For weeks I carried the letter everywhere I went."

"No wonder," James said. "A letter from a real, live president."

"But I've got something even better than that, James," said Mr. Danvers.

He lifted a black book from his desk. Handing it to James, Mr. Danvers asked, "Do you have one of these?"

"Sure, I have a Bible," James said. "But it's not as cool as a letter from a real President."

"Oh, this is much cooler," Mr. Danvers said. "This is a letter from God."

James looked at the Bible. He'd never thought of it as a letter from God.

"The Bible is filled with personal messages from God written especially for you and me," Brad's father explained. "No matter how many times we read it, we always find some fresh message from God."

"You're right," James said. "A letter from God is awesome. But it's too bad God didn't sign it."

Mr. Danvers laughed and said, "Yes, that's a shame."

Your Turn

How is the Bible like a letter from God?

____

____

Prayer

God, I know that the Bible is Your message to me. When I read it, help me understand what You're saying to me. Amen.

WRITE YOUR OWN LETTER FROM GOD

What if God wrote you a personal letter? What do you think God would say to you? Fill in your name in this letter and then write some things God might say to you. At the beginning are a few lines to get you started. Write the rest of the letter on your own. If you get stumped, think about what the Bible says to you.

Dear __________,
The plans I have for you are…
The way I feel about you is…
Today I hope you will…

____

____

____

____

____

____

____

____

____

____

____

____

Your best friend,
God

I can carry God's Word in my heart.

The law of his God is in his heart; his feet do not slip.

– Psalm 37:31

Verses To Go

Gilberto joined his brother Justo at the bus stop. Justo was mumbling.

Gilberto looked at him and said, "You're talking to yourself. I always knew you'd crack up one of these days. I guess today is the day."

"I'm not talking to myself," Justo said.

"Your mouth was making words and you were the only one out here," Gilberto said. "I call that talking to yourself."

"I'm practicing my Bible verse," Justo explained. "Saying the verses out loud helps me remember them."

"Why do you need to memorize verses?" Gilberto asked. "Don't you have a Bible?"

"Sure I have a Bible," Justo said, "but I don't always carry it with me. When I memorize verses it's like I put a piece of the Bible in my heart permanently."

Gilberto shrugged and rolled his eyes.

"Look," said Justo, "what if you were a soldier in the middle of a battle? Hearing God's Word might make you stronger and braver. You can't read the Bible on a battlefield. But you can recall verses if you've memorized them."

"That makes sense," Gilberto said.

"Last week I had that big math test, remember?" asked Justo. "I was really nervous, so right in the middle of the test I whispered to myself, 'I can do everything through him who gives me strength.'"

"Is that from the Bible?" Gilberto asked.

"Philippians 4:13," Justo said.

"Maybe you could help me learn some verses," Gilberto said as the bus came.

"Sure," Justo said. "But don't practice them out loud or people will think you're cracking up."

Your Turn

Name some situations when you might want to know Bible verses by heart.

___

___

Prayer

God, my head is full of so many songs, TV shows and sports stats! But I know there's room for Your Word, too. Help me find the verses I need to know. Amen.

EXERCISING YOUR HEAD

Have you ever memorized a whole chapter of the Bible? Would you like to? Don't worry, it's easier than it sounds. Psalm 117 is the shortest chapter in the Bible. It's only two verses long! You could easily learn it by heart, and it would make a great prayer at meal time. But don't get mixed up and try to memorize Psalm 119. That's the l-o-n-g-e-s-t chapter in the Bible: 176 verses!

Praise the Lord, all you nations;
extol him, all you peoples.
For great is his love toward us,
and the faithfulness of the Lord endures forever.
Praise the Lord.
Psalm 117

I can trust God to listen when I feel bad.

Hear my prayer, O Lord! Listen to my cries for help!
Don't ignore my tears.

– Psalm 39:12 NLT

The Secret Prayer Word

"I don't know how to pray," Donovan said.

"You know how to talk," said his friend Rachel. "Prayer is just talking to God."

Rachel lay down in the fluffy snow and made a snow angel.

"Yeah, that's what everybody says, but I never know what to say. I try to pray and my brain goes blank," Donovan explained.

"Relax," Rachel said, brushing the snow from her clothes. "There's nothing to it. I can teach you to pray with just two secret prayer words."

"Sure you can," said Donovan.

"I mean it," Rachel assured him. "The first word is 'bad'."

"You want me to use a bad word when I pray?" Donovan asked.

Rachel looked at the sky and sighed.

"No! Just start your prayer by telling God everything that's making you feel bad," Rachel explained. "God wants to know about all the tough things."

"God will listen to all that stuff?" Donovan asked.

"Sure," Rachel said. "God loves you and He wants to hear about everything going on in your life. That includes the bad stuff, even the stuff you wouldn't tell anybody else."

"That sounds easy," Donovan said.

"Yeah!" said Rachel. "And you'll feel so much better after you tell God all the stuff that makes you feel bad."

Donovan decided that maybe praying wasn't so hard. He wondered what the other secret prayer word might be.

Your Turn

If God already knows everything, why should you tell stuff to God?

____

____

Prayer

God, I'm not going to keep any secrets from You. Whenever I feel bad I'm going to tell You all about it. Amen.

PUT THE WEIGHT ON GOD

Do you tell God about the bad stuff in your life? You can! God wants to hear all about it. After you share the bad stuff with God, you will feel better just knowing that He cares.

Here's some good prayer advice from the Psalms. The Psalms were written in a language called Hebrew, and they were written without using any vowels. (You know what vowels are: A, E, I, O and U.) Can you add the vowels to this verse so that it makes sense? It's harder than it seems. Good luck!

(The solution is on page 251.)

Cst yr crs n th Lrd

nd h wll sstn y;

h wll nvr lt th rghts fll.

God enjoys sharing the good things in my life.

For you make me glad by your deeds, O Lord;
I sing for joy at the works of your hands.

– Psalm 92:4

The Second Secret Prayer Word

"Praying is easy," Rachel said, "if you know the two secret prayer words. The first word is 'bad'."

Rachel pitched a snowball at the icicles hanging from the roof of her house. Two broke off and fell to the ground.

"Right," Donovan said. "First I tell God all the stuff that makes me feel bad."

Donovan threw a snowball and knocked off three more icicles.

"So what's the second secret prayer word?"

"The second word is 'glad'. First you tell God what's making you feel bad, then you tell God what makes you glad."

"I get it," Donovan said. "It's like saying thank You to God for all the good stuff in life."

"Stuff like snow," Rachel said. "Dogs. Friends. Ice cream. Books."

"Getting an A," Donovan added. "Hitting a home run. Favorite songs."

"Christmas," Rachel said. "Parents. Warm mittens. The zoo."

"The bad stuff and the glad stuff," Donovan said. "That makes it easy to pray. I'll never run out of stuff to talk about if I tell God about all that."

"God will listen to every word you say," Rachel said. "God will help you with the bad stuff, and He will be pleased when you give Him thanks for the good stuff."

What an easy way to pray, Donovan decided. He was feeling glad to have a friend like Rachel.

"Do you know what else makes me glad?" Donovan asked. "Hot chocolate! Let's go ask my mom to make us some!"

Your Turn

Why would God enjoy sharing the good things in your life?

____

____

Prayer

God, help me notice all the blessings You give me everyday. Thanks for filling my life with so many good things and people. Amen.

BAD AND GLAD

Try making up a prayer using the two secret prayer words. It's easy! Just fill in the blanks below. When you're finished, read the prayer out loud to God.

God, here are three things that sometimes make me feel bad:

1.____

2.____

3.____

Please help me handle these things.

And, God, here are five things that make me feel glad:

1.____

2.____

3.____

4.____

5.____

In Jesus' name, I thank you for these good things!

God wants me to pray for others.

Dear brothers and sisters, pray for us.

– 1 Thessalonians 2:25 NLT

Helping Michael

"Mom, it's terrible," Dylan said sadly. "Michael told me his parents are getting divorced!"

"The Cranstons are splitting up?" Dylan's mother asked. "I can hardly believe it. Poor Michael."

"He was crying when he told me," Dylan said. "I feel awful for him. I wish there was something I could do for him."

"You can be his friend," Dylan's mother said. "Michael's going to need someone to talk to, someone who will be there for him. You can do that."

"That doesn't seem like much to do," Dylan said.

"You can pray for Michael, too," Dylan's mother reminded him.

"If I pray hard enough, maybe God will make Michael's parents stay together," Dylan said with excitement.

Dylan's mother hesitated.

"Maybe," she said. "God can do anything. God might help the Cranstons find a way to stay together. Or God might answer your prayer in some other way."

"Like how?"

"God could give Michael the extra strength he needs to get through this. Or even if they get a divorce, God might help them get over their anger and hurt."

Dylan thought about what his mother was saying and decided it made sense.

"There's no way to guess how God will answer our prayers," Dylan's mom told him, "but praying for each other is always a good idea."

"I'm going to tell Michael that I'm praying for him every day," Dylan said. "He might feel better just knowing that."

"I think he will," Dylan's mother said. "You'll feel better, too, because you'll be helping your friend."

Your Turn

Can you think of someone who needs your prayers right now?

____

____

Prayer

Lord, it's easy for me to pray for things for myself. Help me remember to pray for others, too. Amen.

PAUL'S PRAYERS

Oooops! This computer has made a mess of Paul's prayers for his friends in Ephesus. Each sentence is complete, but the order of the words is mixed up. Can you fix each prayer? Write out the correct prayers on the lines below the computer. The solution is on page 251.

That I will with strengthen you pray power God. (Ephesians 3:16)

Faith pray share you may I your that. (Philemon 1:6)

See we again pray to you. (1 Thessalonians 3:10)

May pray be you we that glorified Jesus in. (2 Thessalonians 1:12)

Your enlighten I that heart God pray will. (Ephesians 1:18)

____

____

____

____

Singing to God is another way to pray.

I will praise the Lord all my life; I will sing praise to my God as long as I live.

– Psalm 146:2

Prayer with a Beat

On the drive home from church, Nick asked his brother, "What's your favorite part of the worship service?"

"I love the prayers," Ian said, drumming on his knee with both hands.

Nick rolled his eyes.

"The prayers? My neck starts to hurt from bowing my head so long," Nick said. "I almost dozed off during the prayer today."

"Not those prayers," Ian said. He shifted the drumming to the Bible resting on the back seat beside him. "I love the prayers we sing."

"You mean the hymns?" Nick said. "Those aren't prayers."

"Sure they are!" Ian said. "We're singing to God, aren't we? What's the difference between talking to God and singing to God?"

"Singing is definitely more fun," Nick said.

"That's my point," Ian told him. "Talking to God with music is more fun for me, too. Sometimes just walking down the street I sing a song to God. People see me singing and playing air guitar, and they don't know I'm really praying."

"Hey, I like that," Nick said. "I could hum a little praise song while I'm going to class and it would be like praying."

"Sometimes I just talk to God," Ian said, "and that's cool. But when I add music, my heart gets into the prayer, too."

Ian moved his hands again and began to drum on the headrest of the front seat.

His mother said, "Ian, stop that. You'll give me a headache."

Nick grinned at Ian and said, "I guess Mom doesn't want you to pray in the car."

Your Turn

Why do you think Christians sing so much?

____

____

Prayer

God, You make me so happy that I can't keep it inside. When I sing to You, I hope You like it as much as I do. Amen.

MUSICAL MOVES

You can add music to your prayers and moves to your music. Here are some simple movements based on American Sign Language. Practice them, then add them to your hymn singing.

God Put your open right hand in front of your face as if getting ready to do a karate chop. Start with your hand just above your forehead and bring your hand straight down in front of your face to the middle of your chest. Keep your fingers pointing upwards through the whole motion.

God

Jesus Start with your hands in front of you as if getting ready to clap. With the middle finger of your right hand touch the palm of your left hand. Then with the middle finger of your left hand touch the palm of your right hand. These motions represent nail scars.

Jesus

Love With your hands in fists, cross your forearms in an X over your heart.

Love

Pray With hands open and fingers closed, press your hands together (palm to palm) in front of you at chest level.

Pray

Hallelujah Start with the position for Pray, then pull your hands apart. Close your hands as if holding sparklers in front of you. Then make two small circles with each hand as if waving the sparklers through the air. This is the motion for Pray and the motion for Celebrate. When you put them together it means Hallelujah.

Hallelujah

Cross Cup your right hand in the shape of a C. With that cupped hand draw an invisible line in front of you moving left to right, than a second line moving from up to down, making the shape of the cross.

Cross

Everyone serves Jesus together in the church.

Let us not give up meeting together, as some are in the habit of doing, but let us encourage one another.

– Hebrews 10:25

Making the Team

Brent straightened his tie and brushed his hair. Then he picked up his Bible and walked into the family room.

"We're still waiting on your sisters," Brent's father said.

"I'll wait in the car," Brent told him.

"All right. I'll try to hurry these girls along," Brent's father said. "Caroline, we're going to miss the opening hymn!"

Although they were late every Sunday, Brent loved going to church. Brent's dad said it was hard to be a Christian all on your own, and the church was like belonging to a team.

That made sense to Brent. On a team, people work together and take care of each other. In Brett's church, when one person was in trouble, everybody helped out. When something good happened to someone, everybody celebrated together.

If the church was a team, then the worship hymns reminded Brett of cheers for God, and the choir members were the cheerleaders. The sermon was like getting together in a huddle to hear the game plan, and the preacher was sort of the coach.

Sunday school was like practice between games. Sunday school was the place to ask questions and make sure you knew what was going on. And like a real practice session, sometimes in Sunday school there was joking and kidding around.

Brent's family came out the front door. Just for fun, Brent leaned forward from the back seat and blew the car horn. Caroline made a face, but then she laughed. In fact, everyone was smiling. Brent decided he wasn't the only one who liked going to church.

Your Turn

What do you like best about going to church?

____

____

Prayer

God, thanks for choosing me for Your team. I love being in Your church, and I love the rest of the team. Amen.

GO TEAM!

Here's your chance to be super-creative! Design a jersey for your congregation – your church team. Be sure to figure out both the front and back of your jersey. Should your church name be on the jersey? Your name? A cross or some other symbol? What colors would you use? Use markers, colored pencils or crayons to color your jersey.

Now how about a church team cheer? Here's one some churches might use:
We like music! We like song!
We can sing out loud and strong!

What about your church? What does your congregation do well? Make up a cheer about it and write it here:

___

___

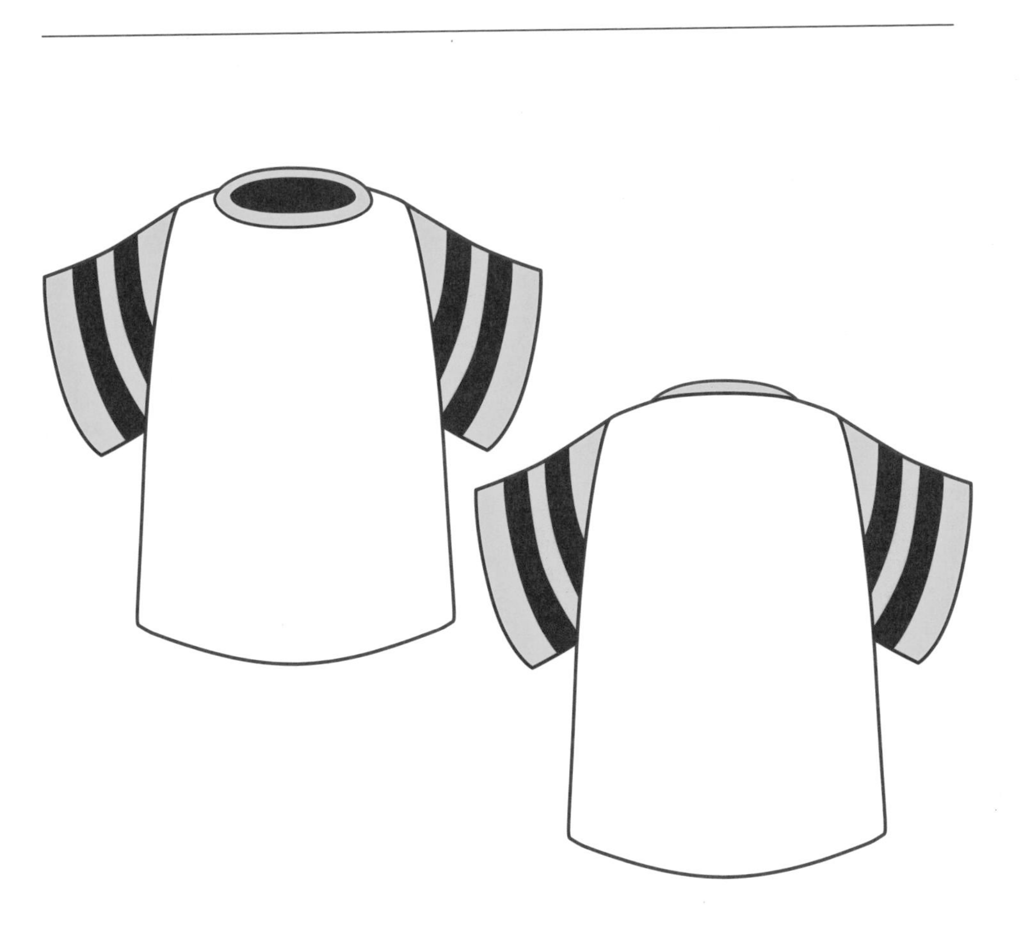

CHURCH

The church helps me serve Jesus.

For we are God's workmanship, created in Christ Jesus to do good works, which God prepared in advance for us to do.
– Ephesians 2:10

Delivery Boy

Austin propped his bike on the kickstand. He went through the door into the church office. Mrs. Sage, the church secretary, smiled as he came in.

"You're always on time," she said. "Every Monday, right on schedule."

Austin said, "My friends would worry if I ran late."

Austin's "friends" were five elderly members of his church–four women and one man. Three of them lived in a nearby retirement home, and the other two lived alone in their own homes. None of the five could come to worship.

Each Sunday the worship service was recorded on tape. Then every Monday after school, Austin picked up copies of the tape and delivered them to the five shut-ins.

Austin's friends loved listening to the tapes. They said it kept them close to the church even though they couldn't come to worship.

They also loved getting visits. Austin never hurried when he delivered the tapes. He made time to talk with his friends. Mrs. Magnus always had two cookies and a glass of milk for Austin.

Mrs. Sage smiled again.

"It's nice of you to do this every week, Austin."

"I'm so glad the church lets me do it," Austin said. "I love having a church job. I thought maybe I was too young to do anything around here, but this job is perfect for me."

"It's not just a job," Mrs. Sage said. "This is your ministry. Every member of the church ought to have a ministry. I'm glad you've found yours."

"Me too," Austin said. "I'd better go. Mrs. Magnus will have cookies waiting for me. I guess that's her ministry."

Your Turn

How is doing a good work a "ministry"?

____

____

Prayer

Jesus, help me find ways to work for You in the church. I'm not too young and I want to help. Amen.

LOVE AT WORK

Jesus healed sick people, fed the hungry and cured the blind. You can't do all the things Jesus did, but you can find ways to help people in your own neighborhood and your own church.

Here are some ideas for things you might do to show the love of Jesus. Put a check mark beside the ones that might fit you. Add others that come to mind.

_______ Bring in mail

_______ Bring in newspaper

_______ Sweep sidewalks

_______ Shovel snow

_______ Rake leaves

_______ Walk a dog

_______ Run errands

_______ Cut grass

_______ Take out trash

_______ Make a visit

_______ Bake cookies

_______ Wash dishes

God cares how I spend my money.

Each [person] should give what he has decided in his heart to give, not reluctantly or under compulsion, for God loves a cheerful giver.

– 2 Corinthians 9:7

The Budget

Jason proudly handed his mother the budget he had worked out. He had started with how much allowance he received each week, and then decided how to use that money. Some of the money each week was set aside for fun, some for his college fund and the rest he was saving for a skateboard.

Jason's mom studied the budget carefully.

"I'm proud of you," she said. "You've done a good job on this, but I don't see the church in your budget."

"Maybe I could give a little to the church after I save enough for my skateboard," Jason suggested.

His mother frowned.

"Have you thought about how much the church does for you, Jason?" his mother asked. "There's Sunday school, Bible school and summer camp."

"So I have to pay for that stuff?" Jason asked.

"No," said Jason's mother. "The church gives you all of that for free. But don't you think you should give something back as a way of saying thank you?"

"If I give money to the church, I'll have less money for me," Jason complained.

"Jason, ask yourself this. If everybody stopped giving, what would happen to the church?"

Jason looked at his budget. He needed some money just for fun with his friends. He knew his college fund was important. And he really wanted a new skateboard. He wanted to help the church, too, but he wasn't sure he had enough money for everything. He wondered what was the right thing to do.

Your Turn

How do you decide how much money to give to your church?

___

___

Prayer

God, I wish I had more money, but I guess everybody does. Show me how I can please You with the money I have. Amen.

GOD'S SHARE

People have different ideas about how much money to give to God's work in the church. Many people believe they should give God 1/10 of all the money they get. What do you believe? The coins below add up to one dollar. Circle the amount of that dollar you think should be given to God.

I am loved at church.

Therefore encourage one another and build each other up, just as in fact you are doing.

– 1 Thessalonians 5:11

The Awful Sunday

Garrett sat in the back seat of the car wishing he didn't have to go to church. He could still remember the embarrassment of last Sunday when he'd messed up his piano part in the worship service.

Garrett had never played in church before. He was nervous when it came time for him to play during the offering. He started out all right, but then he hit a wrong note–a terrible note that stuck out like a bad hair day. That made him more nervous, and then he made more mistakes. Somehow he got through the song, and when he finished he slipped out the door and waited for his family in the car.

That was a week ago. Now Garrett's father parked the car in the church lot and Garrett forced himself to walk into the building. He knew everybody was going to make fun of his piano playing. This was going to be an awful Sunday.

The first person he saw was Miss Grimm, his Sunday school teacher. She beamed at him and said, "Garrett, how wonderful that you played in worship last Sunday. I hope we get to hear you play again soon."

Then Garrett saw Mr. Palmer who sang in the choir.

"Good job last week!" Mr. Palmer said. "I wish I could play piano."

By the time the fifth person told Garrett how much they enjoyed his music last Sunday, Garrett was glad to be at church. He knew he hadn't done a great job at the piano, but these people loved him anyway.

When Mrs. Hall asked Garrett when he was going to play again, Garrett smiled and said, "Maybe next Sunday!"

Your Turn

Does your church feel like a place where you can be yourself? Why or why not?

____

____

Prayer

God, thanks for the church and for the people there who care so much about me. I'm glad to have a safe place where people build me up instead of putting me down. Amen.

THE CHURCH GAME

You need a coin and a game marker (maybe another coin) to play this game. Put your marker at Start. The object is to see how quickly you can get to Winner. You can play with a friend or you play alone and try to beat your best record. To play, put your marker at Start and flip the coin. Move two spaces for heads and one space for tails. Always follow the instructions of any square you land on.

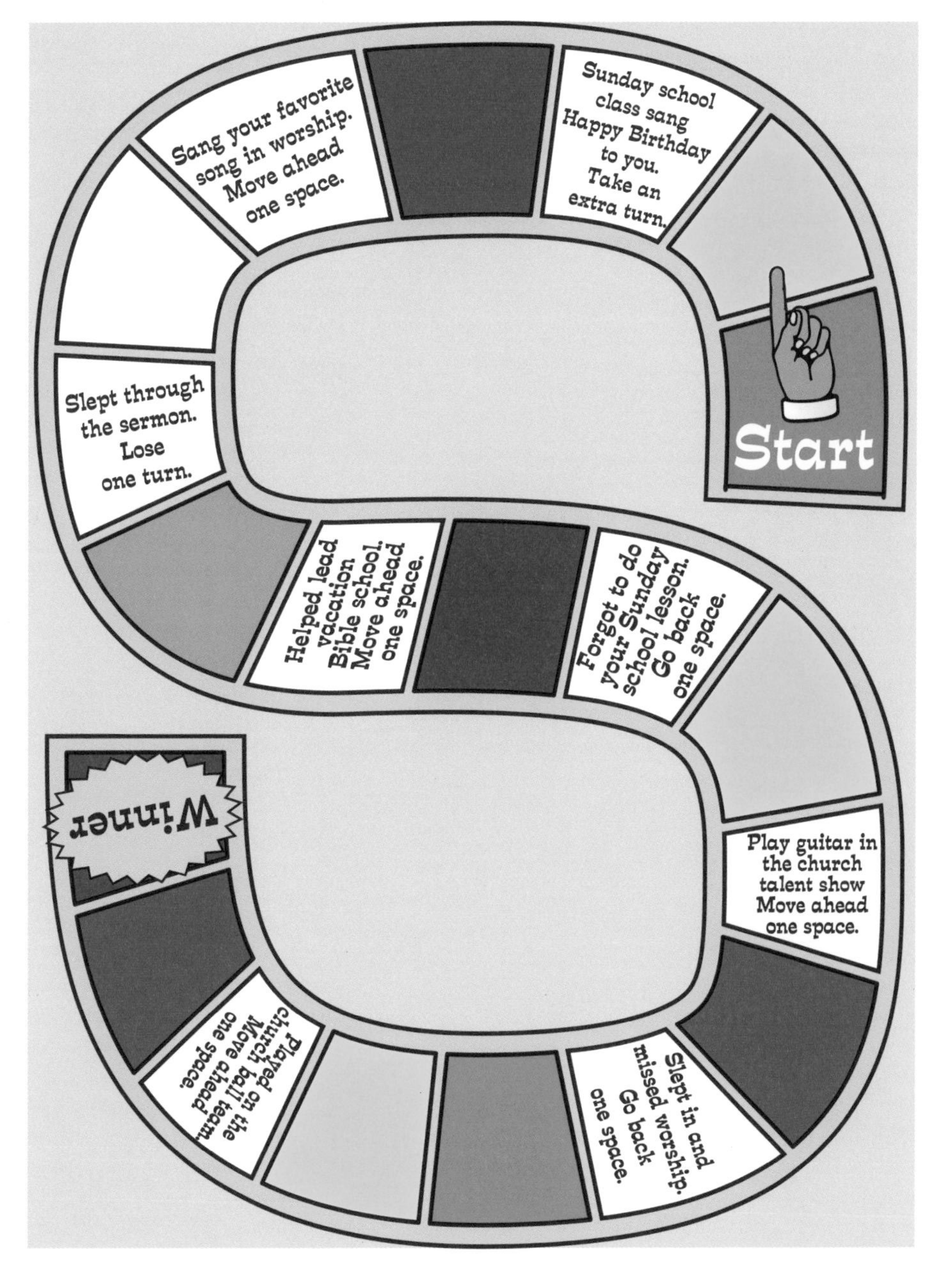

PUZZLE ANSWERS

Page 19

1. Mary Magdalene
2. Simon Peter
3. Cleopas
4. Disciples
5. Thomas

Page 21

Incorrect word:	Correct word:
chickens	sons
fatter	younger
circus	country
flood	famine
window-washer	citizen
pond	fields
ducks	pigs
sardines	pods
cousin	father
smacked	kissed
pet dog	son
hat	robe
tattoo	ring
bells	sandals

Page 29

Ask and it will be given to you; seek and you will find; knock and the door will be opened to you. (Matthew 7:7)

Page 31

He will cover you with his feathers, and under his wings you will find refuge. (Psalm 91:4)

Page 33

1. a, b, d, e
2. a, b, d
3. c, d, e
4. a, b

Page 41

I have hidden your word in my heart that I might not sin against you. (Psalm 119:11)

Page 43

Abraham: "I will give you a land of your own."
Sarah: "I will give you a child."
Moses: "I will bring my people out of Egypt."
Joshua: "I will not leave you or forsake you."
Gideon: "I will help you defeat the Midianites."
Jeremiah: "I will make you as strong as an iron pillar."
Solomon: "I will give you wisdom."

Page 45

1. Bless the Lord, Praise God, Amen
2. Alleluia, Hosanna, Glory to God

Page 55

Page 57
1. C 2. B 3. A

Page 59
Therefore go and make disciples of all nations, baptizing them in the name of the Father and of the Son and of the Holy Spirit, and teaching them to obey everything I have commanded you.
(Matthew 28:19-20)

Page 67

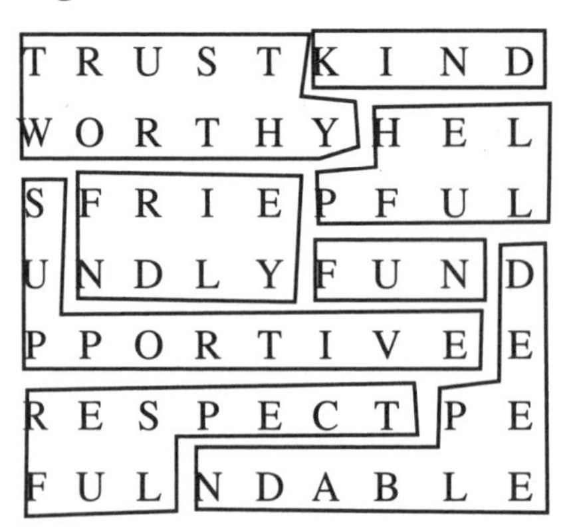

Page 69
Ruth: Woman picking grain from a field
Moses: Old man sitting on rock with man on each side holding the older man's arms in the air
Jesus' Disciples: Fishermen pulling net full of fish onto boat
Paul: One man laying his hands upon the eyes of another
Jesus: Men leading a donkey
A Paralyzed Man: Two people carrying a third person–all standing on roof of house–maybe lowering the paralyzed person through the roof.

Page 71
In love.

Page 75
coins
fish
perfume
wine, water
food
Paul
loaves
cheerful

Page 79
1.J
2.E
3.J
4.J
5.J
6.E
7.J

Page 91
1. Barnabas welcomed Paul and told others Paul could be trusted. He also introduced him in person to the church leaders.
2. Barnabas went to help. He encouraged the new believers. He also sent for Paul so Paul could use his gifts to help the new Christians.
3. Barnabas disagreed with his friend Paul. When Paul wouldn't change his mind, Barnabas planned his own mission trip and took John Mark along.

Page 95
self-control
love
gentleness
kindness
joy
peace
patience
goodness
faithfulness

Page 99
The joy of the Lord
is your strength.
(Nehemiah 8:10)

Page 101
Prince of Peace

Page 109

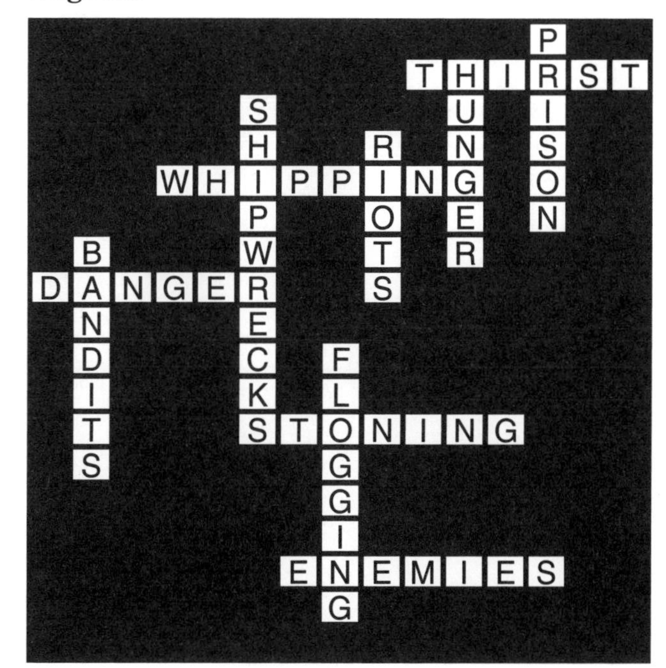

Page 103

Q O X N D **P** V I E N **P** H
T **N** **E** **I** **T** **A** **P** S M D **A** E
D **T** **N** **E** **I** **T** **A** **P** K **T** **T** N
T H D I O **I** N V **N** W **I** N
N H D H U **E** M **E** N G **E** **T**
E N X C O **N** **I** E R Y **N** **N**
I H G A I **T** T Y E F **T** **E**
T F D H **A** N Z I H E N **I**
A H A **P** **A** **T** **I** **E** **N** **T** Q **T**
P **A** **T** **I** **E** **N** **T** F H I H **A**
I V R B Z P I E R M A **P**
P **T** **N** **E** **I** **T** **A** **P** H F S K

Page 117
The Word of God

Page 119
Do not be overcome by evil, but overcome evil with good.

Page 121
He who has been stealing must steal no longer. (Ephesians 4:28)

Page 123
police
bus-driver
teacher
doctor
firefighter
parents
principal
coach
minister

Page 127

Page 125
mercy, love, great, blot, Wash cleanse, sin, know, sin, before truth, parts, teach, pure heart, renew, joy, salvation, willing.

Page 131
The sentences that are NOT scratched out are:
Soccer is important to me, so I never goof off during practice.
I'm too short to get many rebounds, but I'm good at free throws.
My art teacher says my drawing is really improving.
Our softball team is in second place.
If you want, I can show you how to do some pretty good tricks on your skateboard.
The message is: NO BRAGGING!

Page 135
Apply your heart to instruction and your ears to words of knowledge. (Proverbs 23:12)

Page 137
The truth will set you free. (John 8:32)

Page 139
sweat, stone, work, plan, mortar, help, faith, hammer, time, patience

Page 147
The Lord is my shepherd, I shall not be in want. He makes me lie down in green pastures, he leads me beside quiet waters, he restores my soul. He guides me in paths of righteousness for his name's sake. Even though I walk through the valley of the shadow of death, I will fear no evil, for you are with me; your rod and your staff, they comfort me. You prepare a table before me in the presence of my enemies. You anoint my head with oil; my cup overflows. Surely goodness and love will follow me all the days of my life, and I will dwell in the house of the Lord forever. (Psalm 23)

Page 151
No one comes to the Father except through me. (John 14:6)

Page 153
Whoever follows me will never walk in darkness, but will have the light of life. (John 8:12)

Page 155
prayer, obey, Bible, church, worship, love, serve, trust, faith

Page 157

Page 159
The Lord gives food to the hungry.

Page 161
hand, eyes, back, legs, tongue ears. Boxed word: healer

Page 163
Boy with a sack lunch /Helped feed 5,000 people
David/He killed a giant
Jesus/Talked with the wise men in the temple
Samuel/He heard God's voice in the night
Miriam/She guarded her little brother on the river
Joash /Became king when seven years old
Children of Jerusalem/Sang praises to Jesus

Page 171

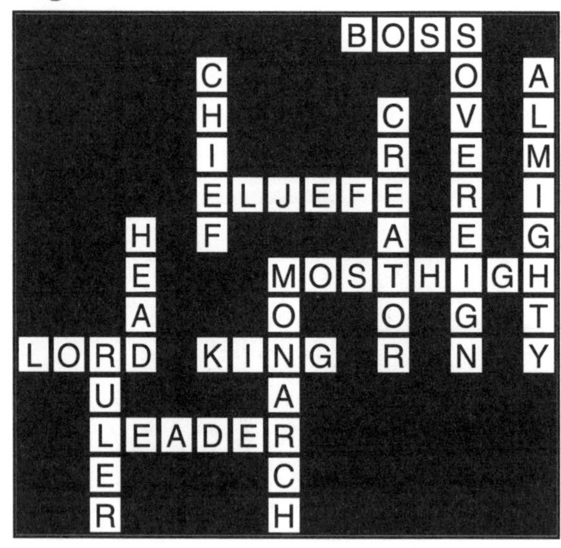

Page 175
tree/sun
robin/worm
dog/bone
shark/fish
rabbit/carrots
boy/hot dog
cow/grass
monkey/banana
bee/flower
venus flytrap/fly
anteater/ant

Page 177

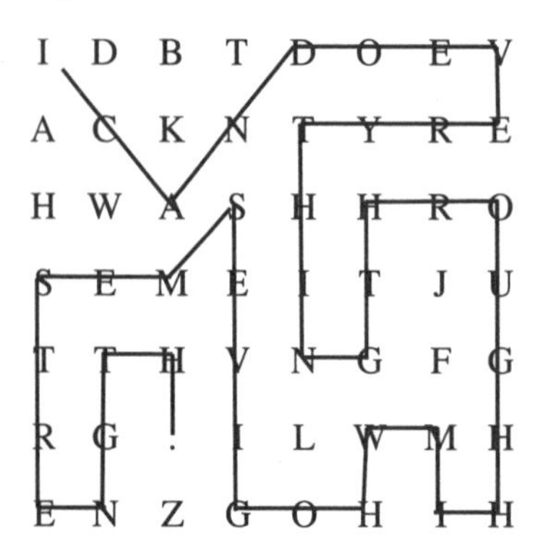

Page 185
Love each other as I have loved you. (John 15:12)

Page 187
God is love.

Page 191
Therefore, if anyone is in Christ, he is a new creation; the old has gone, the new has come! (2 Corinthians 5:17)

Page 201
1. Abram
2. Simeon
3. Noah
4. Moses
5. Sarah
6. Anna
7. Methuselah

Page 203
Do not forget to entertain strangers, for by so doing some people have entertained angels without knowing it. (Hebrews 13:2)

Page 205
He predestined us to be adopted as his sons through Jesus Christ. (Ephesians 1:5)

Page 209
I am making everything new!

Page 211
bee, a spelling bee
fish, scales
camel, a humpback wail
pigs, they are road hogs
horse, a night mare
wolves, they both belong to packs
bull, a bull-dozer
spider, they are always spinning
leopard, one with measles
dog, the outside

Page 215
God saw all that he had made, and it was very good. (Genesis 1:31)

Page 221
Christ is risen from the dead.

Page 223
Commandment 1. gods
Commandment 2. idol
Commandment 3. name
Commandment 4. Sabbath
Commandment 5. father, mother
Commandment 6. murder
Commandment 7. adultery
Commandment 8. steal
Commandment 9. testimony
Commandment 10. covet
Rule 1. heart, soul, mind, strength
Rule 2. neighbor, yourself

Page 229
Cast your cares on the Lord and he will sustain you; he will never let the righteous fall.
(Psalm 55:22)

Page 233
I pray that God will strengthen you with power.
I pray that you may share your faith.
We pray to see you again.
We pray that Jesus may be glorified in you.
I pray that God will enlighten your heart.

FAVORITE BIBLE VERSES

Sometimes when you read the Bible, you'll find a verse or a sentence that really grabs your heart. Use this page and the next to write down those verses so you can have them handy.

FAVORITE BIBLE VERSES